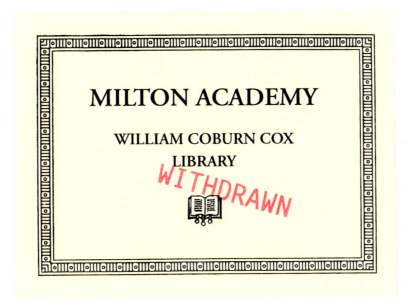

PAPUA NEW GUINEA

Ingrid Gascoigne

 **Marshall Cavendish**
Benchmark

New York

PICTURE CREDITS

Cover photo: © Karen Su / Danita Delimont Stock Photography
alt.TYPE / REUTERS: 38, 57, 76, 92 • Bruce Coleman Limited: 46 • Corbis: 1, 5, 25, 28, 34, 40, 42, 43, 50, 52, 83, 121, 131 • Dave
G. Houser: 8 • Francis Tan: 130 • Getty Images: 22, 29, 32, 37, 56, 58, 66, 78, 111, 114 • Haga Library, Japan: 125, 128 • Hoa-qui
Archives: 23 • Hutchison Library: 35, 113, 118 • Itamar Grinberg: 3, 4, 16, 18, 41, 45, 47, 60, 63, 68, 70, 74, 79, 80, 82, 84, 95, 97,
100, 102, 105, 106, 107, 123, 127 • Lonely Planet Images: 15, 20, 44, 51, 61, 86, 94, 96, 109 • M. MacIntyre / ANA Press Agency:
93, 99, 101, 108, 119 • National Geographic: 48, 91, 104, 110, 112, 120 • North Wind Picture Archives: 21 • Photolibrary.com: 6,
7, 10, 11, 49, 55, 88, 122 • Susanna Burton: 75 • TopFoto: 27, 67, 126 • Travel Ink: 69 • Trip Photographic Library: 14, 17, 36,
53, 59, 62, 64, 71, 72, 77, 87, 103, 117, 124

PRECEDING PAGE
A smiling Papua New Guinean boy steers a boat while his brothers help in the background.

Publisher (U.S.): Michelle Bisson
Editors: Deborah Grahame, Mindy Pang
Copyreader: Sherry Chiger
Designer: Rachel Chen
Cover picture researcher: Connie Gardner
Picture researcher: Thomas Khoo

Marshall Cavendish Benchmark
99 White Plains Road
Tarrytown, NY 10591
Web site: www.marshallcavendish.us

© Times Media Private Limited 1998
© Marshall Cavendish International (Asia) Private Limited 2010
® "Cultures of the World" is a registered trademark of Times Publishing Limited.

Originated and designed by Times Media Private Limited
An imprint of Marshall Cavendish International (Asia) Private Limited
A member of Times Publishing Limited

Marshall Cavendish is a trademark of Times Publishing Limited.

All Internet sites were correct and accurate at the time of printing. All monetary figures in this publication are in U.S. dollars.

Library of Congress Cataloging-in-Publication Data

Gascoigne, Ingrid.
 Papua New Guinea / by Ingrid Gascoigne. — 2nd ed.
  p. cm. — (Cultures of the world)
 Summary: "Provides comprehensive information on the geography, history,
wildlife, governmental structure, economy, cultural diversity, peoples,
religion, and culture of Papua New Guinea"—Provided by publisher.
 Includes bibliographical references and index.
 ISBN 978-0-7614-3416-0
 1. Papua New Guinea—Juvenile literature. I. Title.
 DU740.G36 2009
 995.3—dc22   2008028794

Printed in China
7 6 5 4 3 2 1

CONTENTS

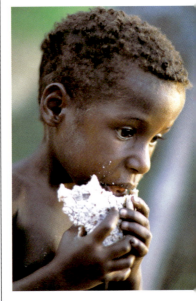

A boy eating sago, a staple food item in Papua New Guinea.

An animal figure and a human figure together make up this totem pole, which belongs to a clan in Papua New Guinea.

INTRODUCTION

PAPUA NEW GUINEA is a young parliamentary democracy that achieved its independence from Australia in 1975. This fledgling nation includes more than 600 small islands and archipelagoes, and its population consists of more than 700 linguistic and ethnic groups scattered across its many islands, living on a diverse terrain of jagged mountains, plains, fertile valleys, and swampland. The country has elaborate oral histories, but they were not recorded until 1526, and the civilization flourished in the heart of its highlands undetected by the Western world until the 1930s. It takes more than a book to describe such a country in detail, but *Cultures of the World: Papua New Guinea* gives a comprehensive overview of a nation that houses hundreds of ancient cultures struggling with development, sustainability, monetization, and modernization in the new millennium.

GEOGRAPHY

PAPUA NEW GUINEA CONSISTS OF more than 600 small islands and archipelagoes, along with the "mainland," the eastern section of the large island known as New Guinea. Situated just south of the equator, it lies to the north of Australia, at the edge of the Pacific Ocean. The Torres Strait—the narrowest point between mainland Australia and Papua New Guinea—is about 100 miles (161 km) across. One of the Australian-owned Torres Strait Islands lies less than 12.4 miles (20 km) from mainland Papua New Guinea.

To the west, Papua New Guinea shares the island of New Guinea with the Indonesian provinces of Papua and West Papua. The Australian and Indonesian governments in 1968 agreed upon the border separating the two countries without consulting the indigenous communities. This

Left: **A settlement of huts beside the Sepik River. Most of Papua New Guinea is forested, and its villages have a remote character.**

Opposite: **A view of the beautiful mountains and grasslands of Papua New Guinea.**

The Papua New Guinean landscape ranges from rugged mountains, tropical jungles, and forested foothills to lowlands, savanna woodlands, mangrove swamps, and flat grasslands.

border has been carefully mapped, but it passes through such rugged areas that little of its length of 482 miles (776 km) is patrolled effectively by either country. There is considerable evidence that people living in the center of New Guinea, including a group of anti-Indonesian guerrillas called the Free Papua Movement, can cross the political boundary at will. To the east lie the Solomon Islands, and to the north lie the Federated States of Micronesia.

The total area of Papua New Guinea is 178,704 square miles (462,841 square km), which is slightly larger than that of California. Of that landmass, about 85 percent is the mainland. The remaining 15 percent consists of islands, the larger of which are New Britain and Bougainville. Some of these islands are the submerged eastern end of a curved mountain chain that begins in the Himalayas and continues through Malaysia and into the Pacific. Some of the islands are within the Pacific Ring of Fire, an area of earthquakes and volcanic activity that forms a large circle in the Pacific Ocean. Others are coral atolls—islands formed by the accumulation of the exoskeletons of many generations of coral. These atolls are usually ring- or horseshoe-shaped and surround a shallow lagoon.

MOUNTAIN RANGES

The mainland is bisected from east to west by a spine of jagged and steep mountains reaching heights of more than 13,000 feet (3,962 m). Temporary paths, such as the Kokoda Track, were cut through the mountains during World War II by factions involved in the fighting, but the ranges are not crossed by a permanent road. The only way to travel between north and south is by airplane or on foot. Despite the isolation, the central highland valleys are among the most fertile and heavily populated areas of the country. The tribal people living there were not discovered by European explorers until as late as the 1930s, and they still maintain a largely traditional way of life. Most of the highland terrain is inaccessible through roads, and European visitors to the region still attract great attention.

In some areas the mountains graduate into rolling foothills extending to the sea, but elsewhere the coastline is largely fringed with mangroves. To the west are large, flat, and sparsely wooded grasslands with abundant rainfall and wildlife.

Despite the mountainous terrain, roads link many towns. The construction of such roads is a difficult and expensive operation. The longest road is the Highlands (or Okuk) Highway, running 380 miles (612 km) from Lae to Mount Hagen in the central highlands and then onto Tari and Porgera.

A view of the meandering Sepik River, which cuts through some of the wildest rain forest jungles in the world. Interestingly, this river is not famous for its length but for its incredible depth. Boasting a strong flow, the depth at the river mouth reaches more than 656 ft (200 m), thus enabling big ships to enter from sea all the way to the inlands.

FAST-FLOWING RIVERS

The mainland is laced with a network of rivers that flow from the central mountains toward the coast. The largest are the 700-mile (1,127-km) Sepik, which heads toward the Bismarck Sea in the north, and the Fly, which flows southward into the Gulf of Papua. These rivers are usually fast flowing and navigable and provide a useful alternative to the rough land routes.

The Sepik is bordered by large expanses of swamp for most of its length. There are few natural resources that can be exploited, so there has been little development. Nonetheless, the Sepik region, which includes the river, its tributaries, and the surrounding villages, is well populated and noted as a center for traditional art. The uppermost reaches of the Sepik, among the most isolated parts of the country, have witnessed little change and remain relatively untouched by Western influence.

LIVING WITH VOLCANOES

Papua New Guinea lies within the volcanic and earthquake belt that circles the Pacific, running through Japan, Indonesia, New Zealand, and New Guinea. Volcanoes are an ever-present threat to the people who live near them, but fortunately they erupt infrequently, and well-planned emergency procedures can save entire populations.

Lava flows very slowly, but although people can outrun it, the lava can do much damage to forests, roads, and buildings. Falling ash can bury entire towns, but this normally happens over an extended period, and ashfall needs to be very thick before it becomes difficult for people to breathe.

On the morning of September 19, 1994, Tavurvur and Vulcan—two volcanoes near Rabaul—erupted without warning. Violent explosions, poisonous gas, and a thick cloud of ash forced nearby residents to evacuate to safety. Vulcan ceased its activity in October of that year, but explosions continued at Tavurvur until March 1995. People were able to return to Rabaul in April 1995, and only five deaths were recorded.

Despite the destruction they cause, volcanoes provide rich soil minerals, and to farmers living in the area, this is a silver lining to the proverbial cloud.

LEGACY OF GONDWANALAND

*"On the mainland
alone, there may
be as many as
20,000 species of
flowering plant."*

—*Neil Nightingale,
in his book*
New Guinea,
an Island Apart.

The island of New Guinea is thought to have once been a part of the supercontinent of Gondwanaland, which included Australia, Antarctica, Africa, and South America. The supercontinent began to break up about 65 million years ago, and many of the plant and animal species found throughout Asia, Australia, the Pacific, and even Africa can be found in Papua New Guinea. There is much contrast between the mountains and the low-lying areas because of the differences in temperature and rainfall, and different plant types have adapted to the conditions at each altitude.

The peaks of the highest mountains are occasionally white with snow, but this is the exception. Above 11,000 feet (3,353 m), the mountains are covered with a type of alpine woodland that is very much like the tundra in North America, with tussock grasses, low shrubs, tree ferns, southern pine, and native cedar. Many of the tiny flowers have close relatives as far away as the Himalayas and the Alps. Lichens and mosses tint the landscape with spectacular hues of white, purple, gray, red, and pink. Some areas can be boggy, and rich organic soils such as peat are widespread.

Farther down the slopes, at an altitude of between 11,000 and 6,600 feet (3,353 and 2,012 m), the montane forests are located. The landscape is similar to the highlands of New Zealand or Scotland, something unexpected on a tropical island. Here conifers and southern beech trees predominate, with an underlayer of large ferns and fungi. A single tree can support up to 400 species of epiphytes (plants that live on a host plant but do not feed off it) such as orchids, mosses, and ferns.

Vegetation is thick throughout most of Papua New Guinea, but at the higher altitudes the trees grow stunted and twisted, in keeping with the dark and gloomy atmosphere. Oak trees and pandani (also called screw pines) are common, giving way to the lower montane forests at above 3,300 feet (1,006 m), where hoop and klinki pines, both valued for their timber, are dominant species. Klinki pines tower over the rest of the forest, reaching heights of more than 280 feet (85 m).

The valleys and lowlands that cover more than 75 percent of Papua New Guinea are primarily tropical rain forest. Massive trees form a canopy, and many palm trees, bamboos, pandani, and canes compete for sunlight. The plants grow rapidly with the high temperatures and ample water supply, and some trees reach 150 feet (46 m) in height. Vines and climbers such as rattan and strangler figs add to the tangle of greenery. These are among the most fertile places in Papua New Guinea; in many valleys and along the low slopes, the villagers clear small patches of ground to grow sweet potatoes and bananas.

In the lowland regions, particularly around the rivers, there are large areas of swampy woodlands. In some areas, the grass appears to float on the constantly sodden earth. The residents harvest sago (a starchy palm used for food), wild sugarcane, and *pitpit* (a sturdy cane used in the building of homes). At the western end of mainland Papua New Guinea and in the drier areas around Port Moresby, the landscape becomes a savanna woodland similar to that of northern Australia. Dry grasses and thinly placed trees, mostly eucalyptus, are found here.

New Guinea and Australia are thought to have been joined as recently as 6,000 years ago. It is not surprising, then, that they share many animal species, particularly marsupials—mammals whose young develop inside pouches found on their mother's stomach. Wallabies, tree kangaroos, bandicoots, possums, and echidnas are found in both countries.

Pandanus nuts are highly valued and take some trouble to collect. People trudge for several days to lay claim to trees in the nutting season. The nuts are tough and heavy, and only a few clusters can be carried at a time. As a result, they are sparse in the markets and quite expensive.

COSMOPOLITAN CAPITAL

Port Moresby has a population of 271,813 people, making it the country's largest town. Sited on a natural harbor, it was formerly the administrative headquarters of British New Guinea and remained so when the territory was amalgamated with Australian New Guinea after World War II. When the country gained its independence in 1975, Port Moresby's status as the capital became more culturally meaningful. The central government offices, Parliament House, the University of Papua New Guinea, the National Museum and Art Gallery, and an international airport are located there.

The national buildings are mostly large, modern buildings spread out on spacious grounds, but Port Moresby has shantytowns, too. People are lured to the city by the seemingly prosperous lifestyle, but many end up living in squalid conditions among the squatters. Violence and crime are high, and gangs of young male bandits called rascals, who operate all over the country, are particularly active in impoverished urban areas with high unemployment.

REGIONAL CENTERS

LAE This town is located more centrally than Port Moresby and has a deeper natural harbor, making it a prosperous shipping center. It has road links with the fertile highlands, where cash crops such as coffee and tea are grown, and has often been suggested as an alternative site for the nation's capital. It has a high unemployment rate among its population of 113,118, however, and petty crime is prevalent.

Mount Lunaman, a hill in the center of town, was the lookout point for the Japanese soldiers during World War II. It is riddled with tunnels and caves that are now occupied by the "rascals." Formerly a supply center for gold mining, the original town was destroyed in the grim battles that were fought to expel the Japanese military during World War II, but Lae has been rebuilt farther inland.

Night view of a monument in Madang.

MADANG With a population of 32,117, it has often been called the prettiest town in the Pacific and is thus geared toward the tourist trade. It is a major northern coastal port that lost much of its business to Lae when the Highlands Highway, running from Lae to the central highlands, opened. It has, however, captured the area's logging trade to support its economy.

WEWAK AND GOROKA These two towns (25,143 and 17,269 inhabitants respectively) were useful to the Europeans as trading points, pawns, and strategic locations during World War II. They have been able to thrive because of trade, attracting a large mix of cultural groups.

Pigs are an integral part of family life in Papua New Guinea.

ON THE LAND

Double-wattled cassowaries are found in New Guinea, most often in the rain forest, though occasionally they stray to swampy, forested areas. Some tribes hunt them for their meat, which is considered a delicacy. Their feathers are used to decorate headdresses, and the feather quills are used for earrings. These animals have been traded throughout Asia for at least 500 years. For some native clans, cassowaries are the subject of legends and believed to have mystical powers. Cassowaries were sought by wealthy European collectors in the 16th and 17th centuries for display in private zoos.

A variety of wild dog similar to the Australian dingo is found in New Guinea. It is seldom seen but can be heard howling at night in the highest parts of Papua New Guinea. Domesticated dogs are kept as pets and to aid in hunting.

Papua New Guinea has varieties of snakes, including the poisonous death adder and taipan. The country is also home to tree kangaroos and other marsupials.

Pigs were brought to Papua New Guinea about 6,000 years ago, most likely by immigrants or traders from Southeast Asia, and they play an important part in the life of a village. While some Papua New Guineans, especially the Seventh-day Adventists, do not eat pigs, other Papua New Guineans feast on them. They treat these animals as an indispensable part of the family. They are spoken to and are given names. Women harvesting sweet potatoes often lead pigs to the fields, where they are let loose to root for remaining tubers. Not only are the pigs fed this way, but they also help to till the soil, which must otherwise be done manually.

IN THE AIR

Papua New Guinea is recognized as having one of the richest and most diverse bird populations in the world, and many of the birds have been declared national animals. There are more species of kingfishers, pigeons, and parrots here than anywhere else. Other birds include hornbills, big palm cockatoos, and cassowaries. The birds feast on the fruits, nuts, nectar, and pollen that in other countries are eaten by monkeys and other primates or squirrels. The most famous bird, which appears on the country's flag and coat of arms, is the beautifully plumed bird of paradise. Of the 43 species of this bird, 38 are found in Papua New Guinea. Its feathers can be seen decorating the elaborate headdresses of the indigenous people.

Perhaps most spectacular of all of Papua New Guinea's fauna is its variety of insects. The largest of all moths, with a wingspan of up to 10.6 inches (27 cm), the Hercules moth is found here. There are also giant millipedes, sticklike insects that reach more than 12 inches (30 cm) in length, and the breathtaking birdwing butterflies. Of the 11 birdwing species documented, eight are found in Papua New Guinea. The female Queen Alexandra's birdwing has a wing span of up to 12 inches (30 cm). Another insect that invites curiosity is the antlered fly, found only in northern Australia and Papua New Guinea. The males of this fiercely territorial species have a large antlerlike structure protruding from their heads, which they use as a defensive display. Some insects, such as green scarab beetles, are used by the natives as body ornaments. Many of the unusual insects are now being collected and bred to ensure their conservation.

The bird of paradise is found mainly in the New Guinea highlands and on nearby islands. It is the adult male of the species that boasts beautiful plumage.

PROTECTED BY THE LAW

Early European and Asian traders were quick to exploit the unusual wildlife, paying local people to hunt for the spectacular and rare hides and feathers, which were then exported and sold for a high price. This quickly decimated many species on the islands.

Much of Papua New Guinea's wildlife is now recognized as a valuable asset, and since the 1920s many species have been declared national animals and protected by legislation. This means they can be hunted only by traditional methods for tribal use. Commercial and sport hunting of these animals is illegal, and the penalties for transgressors are stiff.

Many indigenous communities believe that certain animals represent the spirits of their ancestors and, therefore, that they own the land on which these animals are found. The daily life of the tribal landowners is inextricably tied to their surroundings. There are traditions and laws that conserve the natural resources on which they depend for their livelihood.

The waters surrounding Papua New Guinea nurture beautiful marine life and coral reefs.

IN THE WATER

The coastal areas are lined with swampy marshes teeming with plants that have adapted to living in the salty tidal conditions. They act as a haven for fish and prawns to breed, and in some areas the trees can grow up to 100 feet (30 m) high. The seawater is often heavily silted because of the steep slopes down which the high rainfall flows into the rivers and sea. Divers consider Papua New Guinea one of the best dive sites in the world. The area also provides an ideal habitat for sea grass, a land plant that has adapted to living in the sea. It grows where the water is too deep for mangroves but too murky for coral and supports a huge number of sea creatures, including the dugong, or sea cow.

Several varieties of marine turtle are caught by the coastal people, including the green turtle for its meat and the hawksbill for its shell. Fly River has its own tube-nosed turtle, which can be seen on the country's five-toea coin. Whales, dolphins, corals, venomous sea snakes, and an abundance of yet unclassified marine creatures fascinate divers and marine biologists alike.

ENDANGERED SEA COWS

Dugongs are thought to be one of the creatures that early European sailors mistook for mermaids. These sea cows, as they are commonly called, are large marine mammals that can grow to 9 feet (2.7 m) in length, and a male can weigh up to a ton (1,016 kg). They inhabit shallow coastal waters and are herbivorous, docile in nature, and slow moving. Sea grass is the dugong's primary food. An adult dugong may need to eat up to 88 pounds (40 kg) of sea grass to meet its daily food requirement.

The animals live in pairs or in small groups. They can stay underwater for only two or three minutes before having to surface for air, at which point they become relatively easy targets for hunters. Dugongs are prized within certain Papua New Guinean communities and elsewhere for their meat, blubber, skin, tusklike incisors, and oil. They can no longer be found in many of their former haunts and are now considered a threatened species, with fewer than 100,000 of them left in the world.

WET, HOT, AND HUMID

Temperatures are high in most of Papua New Guinea's lowland areas and along the coast, with maximum temperatures averaging 90°F (32°C). The highland areas are much cooler at about 72–77°F (22–25°C).

For the most part, the country experiences two main seasons, the wet and the dry. However, there is so much rain in some areas that the land is never dry at all but merely less sodden. The northwest monsoon brings rain from December to March, and southeasterly trade winds blow from May to October, bringing drier and cooler weather. April and November are the most uncomfortable times, as these are the transition months.

The intensity of the rainy period varies greatly from one region to another, as the mountains tend to capture much of the precipitation, sheltering some areas from the monsoonal rain. The Port Moresby area has a definite dry season, with an annual average rainfall of about 39 inches (1 m) that occurs in short bursts during the wet season. In Lae the average rainfall is more than 177 inches (4.5 m), falling mostly between May and October, with the wettest months being June, July, and August. In some areas (the western part of New Britain, parts of the Gulf of Papua, and some of the western provinces) there is rain all year round, and rainfall can average more than 236 inches (6 m) per year.

Despite heavy rainfall in the rest of the country, the capital city of Port Moresby is much drier. The effect is particularly evident during the dry season, from May to October, when the city suffers extended conditions of drought and has to impose strict rules on water rationing.

AD MAJOREM DEI GLORIAM
• • •
IN THIS PLACE ARE RECORDED
THE NAMES OF OFFICERS
AND MEN OF THE BRITISH
COMMONWEALTH OF NATIONS
WHO DIED DURING THE
1939-1945 WAR IN THE NEW
BRITAIN AREA, ON LAND, AT
SEA AND IN THE AIR, BUT TO
WHOM THE FORTUNES OF WAR
DENIED THE KNOWN AND
HONOURED BURIAL GIVEN TO
THEIR COMRADES IN DEATH
• • •

HISTORY

THERE ARE NO WRITTEN RECORDS of the history of Papua New Guinea before the arrival of European explorers several hundred years ago, but the country has had a tradition of passing down history orally. The country is a collection of vastly different cultural groups. Even as recently as the 1930s some areas still used tools made of stone and wood. Nevertheless a complex social structure exists within each group. The prehistory of Papua New Guinea has been pieced together largely by archaeologists and anthropologists.

It is widely thought that the first people on the New Guinea mainland arrived as emigrants from the eastern Indonesian islands as early as 50,000 years ago, in the glacial period. Later arrivals came from other areas in Indonesia, Asia, and the South Pacific. These people were hunters and gatherers and were most likely nomadic. Although New Guinea probably was once connected to Australia, part of the immigrants' journey involved crossing deep seawaters in canoes.

It is highly probable that new agricultural methods were introduced by farmers arriving from Southeast Asia. As tools were developed and crops introduced, larger groups of people settled in fixed locations. Archaeological discoveries include drainage channels in the highlands at a site in Kuk Swamp that indicate the existence of agriculture around 10,000 years ago. Trenched roads, defensive gates, and ditches used for fighting have also been found in the southern highlands, indicating that the groups that had settled here were at war with each other. Between 17,000 and 10,000 years ago, climatic warming led to a worldwide melting of ice sheets, resulting in a gradual rise in sea levels, which covered the original land links with Australia. The grasslands decreased in size, and the forested areas increased.

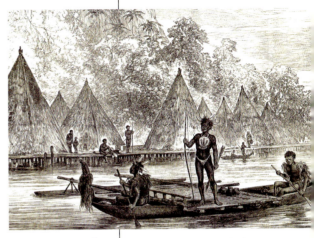

Above: **An artist's impression of the life of the locals in the past. From ancient to modern times, dugout canoes have been used for transporting people and cargo. These are made by hallowing out a tree trunk, usually through burning, chipping, and scraping. Given the narrow water banks of Papua New Guinea, the humble dugout canoe still provides a useful means of travel for tribal people living along the coast.**

Opposite: **A man stands looking at the Bita Paka Commonwealth War Graves memorial near Rabaul. This place acknowledges members of the Allied forces killed in Papua New Guinea during World War II.**

TRIBE AND CLAN AS BASIC SOCIAL UNITS

Unlike in other parts of the world, the development of agriculture in what is now Papua New Guinea did not cause the growth of larger political and social units such as cities and states. Instead the tribe and the clan remained the basic social units. Because the basic food crops could not be stored for long periods due to climatic conditions, it was not possible to stockpile food to create wealth, nor could farmers take time out to fight protracted wars to conquer neighboring territories. Short and ferocious battles were fought over territory and property, but these were conducted mainly in the valleys, with villages built defensively on the hillsides.

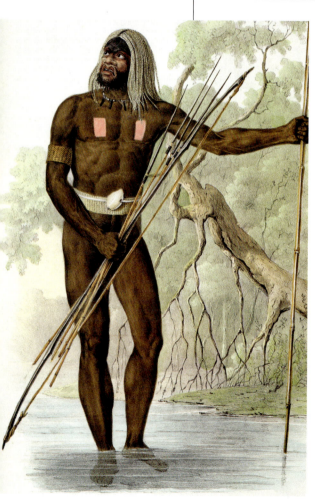

FARMERS AND TRADERS 10,000 YEARS AGO

Evidence suggests that New Guinea highlanders may have been among the world's first agriculturalists, growing crops of yams, bananas, and coconuts. The early farmers developed sophisticated techniques to obtain maximum yields without the use of metal tools, including composting dead vegetation to add nutrients to the soil and a system of crop rotation.

Long before Europeans arrived, overland and interisland trade routes existed for the exchange of sago, pottery, shells, salt, and stone axes. Large seagoing trade expeditions called *hiri* (hih-REE) were launched by the Motu in the Port Moresby area, who traded pots for sago and canoe logs in the Gulf of Papua. In subsequent trade with Asia that lasted 1,000 years, Chinese merchants and sea captains were the middlemen in exchanges of Asian glass beads, metal goods, cloth, and porcelain for New Guinea tree bark, spices, and exotic bird feathers.

Steel axes, which preceded the arrival of European settlers, were traded inland. They were more efficient than stone axes for clearing gardens and making canoes. Use of the steel axes increased leisure time for the men, which eventually led to frequent tribal wars.

EUROPEAN ARRIVAL

Written history in Papua New Guinea began in 1526 when the Portuguese sea captain Jorge de Meneses sighted the coast and named it Ilhas dos Papuas (Land of the Frizzy-haired People). He was unimpressed with what he found—a difficult terrain with no apparent spices or natural wealth to encourage further exploration. The Spaniard Iñigo Ortiz de Retes landed on the northeastern parts of the mainland in 1545 and named the land Nueva Guinea (New Guinea) because it reminded him of the Guinea Coast in Africa. Explorers largely ignored the island, as it lay away from the direct sea routes used at the time.

In 1793 Captain John Hayes led the first European attempt at settlement. He claimed the entire island of New Guinea for Britain. He built a fortified settlement that he called Fort Coronation at the western end of New Guinea. It was used for trading in nutmeg trees, dyewood roots, and teak. The settlement was abandoned the following year after it was flooded by monsoonal rains, attacked by hostile locals, and plagued by tropical mosquito-borne diseases. The Dutch disputed the British claim and laid claim to the western half of New Guinea in 1828. As had happened to the British settlers, however, the Dutch were plagued with mosquitoes and the threat of malaria, and they deserted their outpost, Fort du Bus, in 1835. The Dutch continued to claim sovereignty over the western half of New Guinea but were in reality too distant to monitor the territory.

Traders based in Australia were the next to show interest in New Guinea. Whalers and sealers traded small axes, rum, beads, mirrors, and firearms for pearls, tortoiseshell, coconuts, hardwood, rubber, feathers, and copra. In some areas that were used regularly by trading vessels,

Above: **Fierce battles broke out between the villagers and the Europeans over traditional land areas that were taken by force.**

Opposite: **An 18th century artist's painting of an ancient Papua New Guinea man.**

About 9,000 years ago, large parts of the Wahgi swamp areas in the Western Highlands were drained to create productive farming land, an achievement remarkable for its time.

the local population became accustomed to the traders and learned to barter. This helped European traders set up bases in these areas. Other areas were taken by force. By the second quarter of the 19th century, most of New Guinea's coastline had been charted.

From the 1840s parts of New Guinea, Milne Bay, and the Bismarck Archipelago became recruiting points for people supplying cheap labor to sugar plantations in Fiji, Samoa, and Australia. Conditions at most of the plantations were brutal, and the workers, called blackbirds, were exploited. In the 1870s Christian missionaries began to visit New Guinea and the surrounding islands. Their influence is reflected in the high percentage of Christians found in Papua New Guinea today.

In 1884 Germany claimed the northeastern area of New Guinea and the Bismarck Archipelago, setting up a trading post about 300 miles (483 km) up the Sepik River. Fearing a German move south toward their own coastline, the Australian colonies, which were otherwise independent of each other, got together and collectively pressured the British government to make its presence felt more strongly. That same year the southeastern portion of New Guinea was annexed by Britain.

THE DIFFICULTIES OF EXPLORATION

Very little of the Papua New Guinean mainland was explored by Europeans before World War I, because of logistics problems. A porter could carry only up to 40 pounds (18 kg) of food, which was just enough for one person to live on for 14 days, but this would not have been able to sustain prolonged European exploration of the area. The terrain was difficult, and navigating the rivers was not easy. A relay network was soon set up in which teams of porters ferried food and supplies to inland stores, venturing as far into the mainland as was logistically possible. This system had its limitations, however. The use of planes to airdrop food ended this restriction, and there was a boom in successful exploration from the 1920s onward.

LIFE IN THE COLONIES

The New Guinea Kompagnie initially administered the German colony. It was a trading company accorded the task of developing whatever land it could acquire on behalf of the German government. Germany passed the laws for the new territory, but its administration, development, and local matters were entrusted to the company. The company's main concern was profit. It established tobacco plantations in Astrolabe Bay and coconut plantations elsewhere.

The German government took over the company's rule in 1899, and for the most part the colony continued to be run for its plantations and trade value. The focus was on building roads and setting up administrative controls, but little was done for the local people who provided cheap labor for the German operations. Each village was required to nominate a *luluai* (loo-loo-AY), or headman, authorized to collect taxes, settle minor disputes, report major disputes, and ensure that the villagers obeyed government orders. *Luluais* were assisted by *tultuls* (TUHL-tuhls), who acted as interpreters and go-betweens. By 1908 the coconut plantations were maturing, copra exports boomed, and scientific expeditions had

New Guineans under German and Australian colonial control were treated with disdain. They were expected to call all white people Masta *(MAS-tah) or* Misis *(MISS-sis), while a New Guinean male was addressed as* boi *(BOY). They had to stand up when spoken to by a European and step aside when meeting a white person in the street.*

started to penetrate the inhospitable interior. Most of the territory was under the control of government stations and district officers. In 1914 Australian forces occupied the colony, and Germany lost control of it. In 1921 the League of Nations gave Australia mandate over the area, which was renamed the Territory of New Guinea.

When the British had annexed the southeastern area of New Guinea, including Port Moresby, in 1884, their immediate concern—like that of the Germans—had been to set up a governmental infrastructure within the new colony. Their administrative structure was similar to that of the Germans, only instead of having *luluais*, the British established an armed constabulary into which Papuans were inducted as village constables. The area was divided into three divisions, each governed by a regional magistrate. The British protectorate was handed over to Australia in 1906, when it was renamed Papua. After World War I, Australia continued to govern both Papua and the Territory of New Guinea. Administrative control was based in Australia, where all the major decisions were made. These were then implemented by a mostly expatriate Australian staff located in Port Moresby and Rabaul.

GOLD RUSH

In the 1920s gold was found at Wau and Bulolo, and the exploration of the highlands began in earnest. The fledgling use of airplanes in the supply network meant that expeditions could venture farther into the inaccessible and more rugged territories than was previously possible. Around this time, a couple of Australian gold prospectors stumbled upon the New Guinea highland people in a valley. The Australians were astonished to find a civilization of nearly 1 million people who remained untouched by the outside world. Despite the flurry of activity caused by gold mining, little infrastructural development took place during the decades preceding World War II.

CAUGHT UP IN A FOREIGNERS' WAR

World War II arrived in the Papua and New Guinea territories in 1942. The invading Japanese planned to take Port Moresby and set it up as their southern outpost in Southeast Asia and the Pacific, to supply raw materials such as tin, rubber, and oil. The Japanese invasion in January 1942 was swift; the army quickly captured much of New Guinea's north coast and most of the surrounding islands. The Australian and American forces held on to Milne Bay and a few offshore islands, such as the Trobriands. However, the Japanese victory was short-lived. They came close to their original goal of Port Moresby but were driven back by Australian forces at Kokoda.

Soldiers evacuating an injured member during World War II. The Australians fought hard against the advancing Japanese troops in Papua New Guinea.

By September 1942 the Japanese had started their long, slow retreat. It took the Allied forces till 1945 to recover the mainland, and some islands were not reclaimed by Australian forces until after the atomic bombings of Hiroshima and Nagasaki.

The war fought in Papua New Guinea was a particularly grim one. The soldiers traveled through the rugged and seemingly impassable terrain largely on foot and with minimal supplies. By 1942 the warring countries took to the air in an attempt to hasten their victories, starting a series of bombing raids that continued for three years. The devastating effects of war were widely felt by the local people—the bombardment of their towns and villages resulted in the destruction of canoes, trees, plants, and animals that they depended on for their livelihood. The danger of aerial attack and military restrictions on sea travel limited coastal fishing. The scarcity of food and other raw materials added to the hardship of living in a country at war.

An estimated 55,000 indigenous Papuans and New Guineans were involved in World War II as carriers, stretcher-bearers, laborers, and guides.

27

Britain's Prince Charles at the 1975 Papua New Guinea independence ceremony.

TOWARD INDEPENDENCE

In 1945 Australian colonel Jack Keith Murray was appointed the chief administrator of both territories, now called the Territory of Papua and New Guinea. His task was to establish health and education services, control local disputes, and liaise with plantation owners.

From 1946 Australia administered the territories under a United Nations mandate. Soon after, the push toward independence was set in motion. The First House of Assembly was formed with 64 members in 1964. This was replaced in 1968 with the Second House of Assembly, with 94 members. The Second House decided that the independent country would be known as Papua New Guinea. It set up a committee in 1972 to draft a constitution, and the Third House of Assembly was formed. On December 1, 1973, the territory obtained full self-government, and on September 16, 1975, the new constitution took effect. Prime Minister Gough Whitlam of Australia and Britain's Prince Charles attended the official change of flags, along with a crowd of 10,000 people in a stadium in Port Moresby.

POSTINDEPENDENCE

Not everyone in Papua New Guinea agreed that independence was a good thing. There was the problem of creating a sense of loyalty to the central government, located far away from many in Port Moresby. To many people,

the highlanders in particular, the government seemed removed from the day-to-day issues affecting them. In a sense, people in the remote villages were fearful of being dominated by others with a lifestyle that was more advanced. Some areas of the country were officially barred to travelers because of possible hostility of the indigenous people and cannibalistic practices. Since independence, the establishment of local governments and village courts has done much to ease the tension.

However, the failure to create a sense of national identity has resulted in numerous separatist movements that flare up periodically. In 1972 Josephine Abaijah, the first woman to be elected to the House of Assembly, pushed for the southern region of Papua to break away from the rest of the country and declare its independence. She was supported by many wealthy businesspeople of the region who did not want to share their region's affluence with the rest of the country.

A man from the Tari tribe in the Southern Highlands Province of Papua New Guinea looks toward his hut home. The Australian administration of the Territory of Papua and New Guinea faced the challenge of honoring promises it had made to respect local customs and safeguard traditionally owned land while providing profit incentives to attract Europeans with expertise and capital.

District or provincial officers travelled deep into the mountainous areas to educate villagers on modern ways. They explained how the government operated and how it wanted to keep diseases in check and help the people grow better crops. The officers faced the possibility of attack from indigenous warriors and had to work hard to win their trust and goodwill.

TROUBLE ON BOUGAINVILLE

Proponents of the secessionist movement on Bougainville Island argued that the island had stronger cultural and geographic ties with the Solomon Islands than with New Guinea. In 1964, Panguna—one of the locales on the island—was the site of a major copper discovery. More than $288 million was invested in the development of the mine and the surrounding infrastructure including roads, a new town, a power station, and a seaport. By the time Papua New Guinea gained its independence, the mine was earning half of the country's internal revenue.

When the secessionist movement headed by Father John Momis escalated in 1976, negotiations were held. The secessionists were assured they would exert a strong influence on the rest of the country and were allowed to set up the first provincial government. Thus persuaded, they reluctantly chose to remain within the jurisdiction of the national parliament, and things seemed well for a short time.

A small group of traditional landowners enjoyed huge royalties from mining, but little community development resulted. There was growing suspicion among the people that they had been shortchanged in their

NATIONAL FLAG

The flag of Papua New Guinea was formally adopted in 1971. It is based on a design by a 15-year-old student, Susan Karike, winner of a national competition. Black, red, and yellow are traditional colors. The yellow bird of paradise, which features widely in tribal activities, soars above the Southern Cross, symbolizing the country's evolution into nationhood. The Southern Cross, a constellation found in the Southern Hemisphere, signifies Papua New Guinea's historical links with Australia and its goodwill toward its South Pacific neighbors.

earliest negotiations with Bougainville Copper Limited's parent company, CRA. In 1987 the Panguna Landowners Association was formed, led by Perpetua Sereo and Francis Ona. It demanded stricter environmental measures, back payments in profits, and $10 billion in compensation. When CRA failed to meet these demands, the Bougainville Revolutionary Army began to sabotage the mine, which was closed in May 1989. This was a blow to Papua New Guinea's economy, though it was partially offset by the Ok Tedi copper and gold mine and other highland mines. A state of emergency was declared, and the situation deteriorated into civil war.

Early in 1997 the prime minister, Sir Julius Chan, and a few cabinet ministers hired a London-based mercenary group, Sandline Limited, at a cost of about $36 million, to fight the Bougainville insurgents. Neither parliament nor the people were consulted. In March Brigadier-General Jerry Singirok, who spoke against the move, was fired for insubordination. The issue aroused national outrage marked by violence in the capital. Riot police were sent in, the Sandline contract was suspended, and the prime minister and his deputy resigned.

In the 14 years from Papua New Guinea's independence in 1975 to Bougainville Copper's closure in 1989, Bougainville Copper provided a massive 20 percent of the government's total revenue.

PEACE AND LIMITED AUTONOMY

Meetings between Bougainville factions were held on neutral territory in New Zealand. A cooperative agreement was signed in 1998, recommending a ceasefire, total demilitarization of the area, and the establishment of an international peacekeeping force. The process culminated in the Bougainville Peace Agreement in 2001, with Bougainville being given immediate but limited self-government. Some 20,000 people died before peace was achieved. The first elections for the autonomous Bougainville government were held in 2005, and on June 15, 2005, the new 39-member parliament was sworn in, with Joseph Kabui as the first president. A referendum will be held no less than 10 years and no more than 15 years from this date to determine whether Bougainville will become an independent state. The Panguna mine remains closed.

GOVERNMENT

PAPUA NEW GUINEA IS AN INDEPENDENT STATE and a constitutional monarchy at the same time. The situation is the same as in countries such as Canada, New Zealand, and Australia. Independence means that Papua New Guinea is self-governing, formulates its own laws, and has its own government. Yet it is a member of the British Commonwealth, with the British monarch as its head of state. The monarch, currently Queen Elizabeth II, is represented within the country by a governor-general, whose role is primarily ceremonial. The governor-general must be a citizen of Papua New Guinea.

The nation's democratic structure rests on a popular vote and the right of parliament to lodge a motion of no confidence in the ruling government, resulting in a new election. The 1975 constitution vests executive power in the National Executive Council headed by the prime minister, who is the leader of the majority party in the single-chamber National Parliament. The prime minister subsequently chooses ministers from within his or her political party or coalition of parties.

Opposite: **Some men from the Tari tribe dance on the steps of Papua New Guinea's Parliament House in Port Moresby. The traditional designs on the structure illustrate how the country is determined to tie in the old traditions with their modern society.**

VIKTOR YUSHCHENKO

The National Parliament is the top rung within the three-tier government system—national, provincial, and local—which is similar to that of Australia. Elections are held not more than five years apart. Citizens over the age of 18 are eligible to vote and stand for office in the 109-member parliament and in the provincial and local assemblies.

The National Parliament holds ultimate authority over the provincial and local governments. Parliament can vote to veto provincial or local laws that it decides are not in the best interests of the country. It can also suspend those governments in cases of gross mismanagement. The constitution can be altered only by the National Parliament in two votes of 72 or more members, in two sessions held no less than six weeks apart. The National Parliament is housed in Port Moresby, the National Capital District.

LOCAL COUNCILS

The local councils represent the most fundamental level of government. More than 160 councils preside over issues of regional concern. In isolated areas the councils are more involved with the populace than a faraway political body could possibly be. The councils are responsible for the maintenance of roads, bridges, and markets; the provision of fresh water, sanitation, and public transportation services; and the smooth operation of airfields and postal and other communications in isolated areas. To fund their activities, registration fees are charged on items such as bicycles and dogs, and taxes are levied on land ownership and wages.

The system of decentralized provincial government was introduced in 1976 to quell secessionist uprisings on some of the islands.

POWER TO THE PEOPLE: DECENTRALIZATION

Papua New Guinea's constitution recognizes the importance of involving people at all levels of society in decision-making processes to provide a sense of cohesion. This has resulted in the adoption of provincial and local governments.

Apart from the National Capital District, which is Port Moresby, there are 19 provinces throughout the country, 18 of which have a provincial assembly, an executive council, and a centrally appointed governor who represents the provincial government in the same way that the prime minister heads the national government. The provinces are Central, Oro, Milne Bay, Morobe, Madang, Manus, East Sepik, Western, Sandaun, Gulf, Eastern Highlands, Western Highlands, Southern Highlands, Simbu, Enga, East New Britain, West New Britain, New Ireland, and Bougainville.

Bougainville now has its own autonomous Bougainville government, with a 39-member parliament led by a president. The national government reserved 17 powers, but there are 57 other areas of law where Bougainville can eventually take control after applying for the power from the national government. This province has its own judicial system including supreme and high courts.

The provincial governments deal with social, health, and educational matters and the establishment of village courts in their own regions. They also provide input to the National Parliament on issues relating to community development, mass communications, and the establishment of provincial courts. The provincial governments are funded by a variety of grants from the national government, as well as by taxes from retail sales and the issue of gambling and liquor licenses.

COURT SYSTEM

The judicial system of Papua New Guinea is similar to the U.S. and Australian models. A judge decides the outcome of a case after hearing legal representation from both sides, while more serious crimes are brought before a jury. There are several levels in the court system. The Supreme Court is the country's highest court and the final court of appeal, having the authority to interpret and enforce the constitution. Usually three judges sit together during a hearing in this court. The National Court has unlimited jurisdiction, involving a single judge sitting for each hearing. District courts and local courts have more limited powers and are presided over by full-time magistrates. The village courts hear cases such as robbery or assault within the village. The villagers choose their magistrates, who are not required to have legal qualifications.

Other elements of the judicial system include land courts, which settle disputes over traditional landownership, and administrative bodies that

A group of modern-dressed local men. The village court magistrate is elected from within a village and need not have legal qualifications. As a result, the rulings of the village court sometimes reflect the local standards of what is considered proper behavior, even if these are different from national law.

LAW AND ORDER

The age-old custom of intertribal fighting and the seeking of vengeance has not been wiped out, especially among tribes and clans in the more remote areas that have had little exposure to outsiders. Although warriors who kill in tribal warfare can be tried in a court of law, a village will not necessarily cooperate in the arrest of one of its members. Tribal custom does not regard this as a breakdown of order but the process by which the customary rules of law and order are implemented. As long as a man's action does not affect his own village adversely, his community usually does not regard it as wrong or deserving of punishment. Sometimes a man may refrain from cheating someone from his village but may rob his rival clan. For this offence he will not be punished by his fellow clan members. The rules of behavior that are upheld within a community will not necessarily be upheld outside it.

Chieftains such as this one from the Trobriand Islands have a responsibility to ensure that their tribal members conform to government laws.

control the appointment of judges and magistrates. The discretionary use of the death penalty was reintroduced in 1991 for crimes of rape or murder, but no one has been executed since 1957. The courts are kept busy, particularly with petty crimes committed by the "rascals." Records show that in 1990 the National Court heard more than 1,500 cases, and an estimated 120,000 cases were heard in the district and local courts.

Corruption within the government is another issue that has plagued the country since independence. There is a courtlike organization called the Leadership Tribunal to examine charges of corruption against elected officials. In 1991 Deputy Prime Minister Ted Diro and Governor-General Sir Vincent Serei Eri were compelled by the tribunal to resign when Diro was found guilty of corruption and Eri refused to remove him from office.

The assemblies and courts of law in Papua New Guinea face a distinct challenge, as a significant portion of their participants cannot read or write, and many speak mutually incomprehensible languages. The provision of interpreters and audio recordings of procedures means that more people can be engaged in the legal and political operation of their community.

HIGH TURNOVER OF POLITICIANS

From independence until 2002, candidates were elected on a first-past-the-post system, meaning that the person who received the most votes was elected, even with as little as 15 percent of the votes. This led to claims of corruption and bias, and dissatisfaction sometimes spilled over into postelection violence. Few members had the continuing popular support to last more than one term in parliament, and the high turnover of politicians resulted in a dearth of experience and continuity. National elections are now run on a limited preferential voting system. Voters select their first, second, and third choices, and the first-choice votes are counted. If there is no clear majority, the candidate with the least votes is eliminated, and the preferences from those ballot sheets are distributed. The votes are counted again, and this process is repeated until there is a clear majority. This system was first used for a general election in 2007.

The country's first prime minister, Sir Michael Somare, was faced with the task of building a nation from a great diversity of cultures and languages.

Unlike in the U.S. and Australian systems, the candidates do not stand for election on an ideological platform but instead rely on their personality and regional ties to secure votes. Once in parliament they decide which alliance or party they want to support. The politicians are free to change their party allegiance at any time, depending on the issue being debated and the charisma of the main proponents. In trying to achieve a majority vote on any issue each party attempts to lure members into its camp, and much of a politician's time is spent in political maneuvering, forming and breaking alliances. The drawback is that the shifting alliances of party members cause much instability.

PRIME MINISTERS SINCE INDEPENDENCE

1975   Michael T. Somare (Pangu Pati)
1980   Sir Julius Chan (People's Progress Party)
1982   Michael T. Somare (Pangu Pati)
1985   Paias Wingti (People's Democratic Movement)
1988   Sir Rabbie Namaliu (Pangu Pati)
1992   Paias Wingti (People's Democratic Movement)
1994   Sir Julius Chan (People's Progress Party)
1997   Bill Skate (People's National Congress)
1999   Sir Mekere Morauta (People's Democratic Movement)
2002   Sir Michael Somare (National Alliance Party)
2007   Sir Michael Somare (National Alliance Party)

Sir Julius Chan was one of the leading figures in Papua New Guinea's volatile political scene.

The prime minister is elected by majority vote in parliament and is usually the chosen leader of the majority party or coalition—an alliance formed by mutual agreement between two or more groups with different interests. There is remarkable ideological consensus among the political parties, with only the best means to the end being debated. However, the continually shifting web of alliances means that any prime minister committed to reform is unable to take tough measures if he or she wishes to remain in power.

Changes in legislation do not necessarily affect the ruling government's policies, and the National Parliament can challenge the government with a vote of no confidence. Fortunately the government is protected from such a motion for the first 18 months after a general election. This time frame was formerly six months, but the rapid changing of governments meant that very little could be achieved by any leader. While this highlights the inefficiency of the system, it also means that no political group in the country is powerful enough to stage a national military coup.

It is perhaps surprising that a nation made up of people and leaders with such great differences in culture and language can function smoothly. In a debate in the National Parliament interpreters have to be relied on. Yet in spite of the difficulties, the country operates under a single united and democratic government. In this respect Papua New Guinea has succeeded where some other developing nations have failed.

NATIONAL DEFENSE

The Papua New Guinea Defence Force was created in 1973 while operating under the auspices of the Australian Defence Force. When its command was internalized in Papua New Guinea in 1975 it was merged into a single unified force. It does not have separate army, navy, and air forces but consists of three distinct operational elements: land, maritime, and air, which are supported by training, maintenance, transportation, and supply units within the force. Total military personnel numbered 3,100 in 2004.

The Papua New Guinea Defence Force has been employed both internally and externally. Within the country it patrols the border with Indonesia to prevent border crossings by rebels. Its external involvement arose in 1980 when it was deployed to put down a secessionist movement on Espiritu Santo, an island in the southwest Pacific. On more than one occasion, it has been used alongside the Papua New Guinea police force to maintain control during local uprisings, such as the insurrection movement on Bougainville and when civil unrest arose in Port Moresby in 1997 because of political tensions.

ECONOMY

A LARGE PART OF PAPUA NEW GUINEA'S POPULATION still lives in a largely nonwage system. Up to 85 percent of the people make their living through subsistence farming, obtaining other goods through barter or by selling small amounts of surplus produce. Cash is increasingly used, however, for buying clothes, beer, tobacco, rice, and canned fish and for paying taxes. Money is also needed to pay for children's education.

There is an increasing need for wage-earning jobs as the population grows. More people are being educated and thus becoming employable, but the number of job opportunities remains low. About a fifth of those who work for wages are employed in government services (based largely on the Australian model), and the remainder are engaged in mining for multinational companies, work on plantations or in service industries, or are involved in limited manufacturing. This sector is supported mainly by export earnings, with the principal exports being crude oil, gold, copper, forestry products, palm oil, coffee, and cocoa.

Despite the government's setting of a national minimum wage, the average wage remains low, and 37 percent of the population live below the poverty line. The condition of poverty is defined as income insufficient for one's material needs relative to the standards of living in a society at a specific time.

Left: **A store vendor stands among her beautiful woven textiles.**

Opposite: **As well as appearing on government buildings, traditional motifs cover financial structures such as the Papua New Guinea Bank building in Port Moresby.**

PLENTIFUL NATURAL RESOURCES

Papua New Guinea's hopes of economic development rest on its vast resources of minerals, oil, and natural gas. Mining contributes about 75 percent of the country's export income, and recent expansion in oil and natural gas projects along with a boom in world resource prices have resulted in significant growth in the economy. Gold, copper, and oil compete as the country's biggest earners, depending on fluctuations in world commodity markets. Oil, gas, nickel, silver, and other minerals are the targets for extensive exploration and mining. The government has bargained shrewdly with the multinationals that invest in the various mining projects, winning government and local shareholdings and significant compensation for traditional landowners.

Machinery at work in the mountains of Papua New Guinea. These naturally bountiful gold and copper mines are a good source of revenue for the country.

MINING REGULATIONS

Papua New Guinea law provides for 1.25 percent of a mine's gross export sales to be paid in royalties, 20 percent of which goes to the traditional landowners and the remainder to the national government, which in turn gives the provincial government a grant from national revenue. The landowners are provided with equity in the mining company, and compensation is paid to them according to a set schedule. This is based on the area of land affected, the number of trees cut, the amount of gardens destroyed, and the number of fish and other wildlife driven away as a result of mining activities. In addition, the mine is usually required to offer contracts for spin-off businesses to the local people.

Each mine must negotiate other agreements in a forum, and proposals concerning the relocation of housing or education near a mine must be agreed upon before mining can proceed. Despite this often laborious process, ongoing mining operations can cause much dissatisfaction that spills over into civil unrest. The continued dumping of toxic waste from the Ok Tedi mine into the Fly River and the resulting environmental degradation is an example.

These oil workers are drilling through the earth of the jungle into the oil-bearing core. Even though oil provides the country with a good source of income, it poses a threat to the environment.

A local fisherman arranges his net before going out to fish.

UNTAPPED FISHERIES AND EXPLOITED FORESTS

Fishing has always been a significant activity in Papua New Guinea, which has 5,154 miles (8,295 km) of coastline, large rivers, and more than 600 islands. Fishing is carried out mainly by coastal villagers using traditional methods, a few foreign trawlers licensed to fish in the waters, and a fleet of tuna boats. The tropical waters support a variety of fish including tuna, Spanish mackerel, and barramundi. The lack of processing and canning facilities, however, does not allow this resource to be fully exploited to cater to the needs of the population.

The forestry industry has been active in Papua New Guinea since before independence. Inadequate laws and lack of monitoring by the authorities have resulted in virgin rain forests being torn apart with little regard for conservation of the environment. Such destruction has resulted in land erosion, rivers choked with silt, and a loss of wildlife. It has also affected the rural people who use forest resources for building, food, and medicine. Nonetheless, forestry has long been an export earner, with a large variety of high-quality hardwoods being harvested. These are sold as logs, lumber, and woodchips.

MANUFACTURING

Manufacturing remains a weak area of the economy despite the government's attempts to promote expansion. The problems include a largely unskilled labor force, a lack of vocational training facilities, low productivity, relatively high minimum wages in the urban areas (compared with those in some Asian countries), limited cash resources in the economy, a limited local market to sell to, and competition against cheap imports (because of the strength of the Papua New Guinea currency, the kina, against external markets).

Papua New Guinea produces beverages and processed foods on a small scale for domestic consumption but imports most of its food items.

The isolation of many communities means that the high cost of transporting goods to or from their area outweighs the local desire to possess them. One area of concern is the country's dependence on imported food. Papua New Guinea imports a huge 96.9 percent of the grains consumed, mainly rice, and almost all of its processed foods. It could be producing more of its own food—for example, by canning more fish. The difficulty seems to lie in the lack of local capital to establish industrial facilities, along with a deep-seated reluctance to accept an industry that is largely funded by overseas investors.

Some processing of export agricultural items such as coffee, palm oil, and timber takes place, and there are a few clothing and metal fabrication factories. Beer, cigarettes, and soft drinks have been produced in the country since before independence, and a sugar industry was developed in the early 1980s. To protect the local sugar industry, sugar imports, once banned, are now heavily taxed. Papua New Guinea is self-sufficient in chicken and chicken-based products, and meat canneries have been established in Madang and Port Moresby, but these are not enough to sustain the protein requirements of the whole country. Some areas no longer have the forest resources to support protein supply, and people in some communities cannot afford to buy canned meat.

An agricultural worker tends to vegetables at a commercial farm.

FARMING

As well as creating a livelihood for 85 percent of the population, agriculture plays a very important part in the economy. It provides 40 percent of exports and makes up 35 percent of the gross domestic product. It is estimated that more than 2 million Papuan New Guineans, or about a third of the population, are farmers. There are two distinct types of farming: subsistence farming, the small-scale cultivation of food for sale in the markets, and cash cropping. Subsistence farming means that a family grows only enough food to feed itself. Cash cropping is the cultivation of crops such as coffee and palm oil for sale.

Unlike other developing nations that rely heavily on single cash crops and suffer repercussions when the crop fails or when the world market crashes, Papua New Guinean farmers have a strong subsistence base to fall back on. Many villagers move in and out of cash cropping when they have a need for income and return to subsistence farming when that need is somewhat met. Village root crops (sweet potatoes, yams, and taros) grow quickly and produce a high yield of food energy for the amount of work put into their cultivation, so that time and energy can be devoted to other crops or income-generating activities at the same time. These include selling betel nuts, extra vegetables, meat, fish, or hand-made items.

While much of the country's agriculture is carried out by individuals on small plots of land, there are about 650 estates or plantations of more than 125 acres (51 ha) each. While the trend is toward Papua New Guinea ownership, 30 percent of plantations are still owned by church missions. Their workers are largely unskilled and paid a low wage.

CASH CROPS

Coffee, palm oil, and cocoa are the most important cash crops. Copra, the dried flesh of the coconut from which coconut oil is extracted, was a major contributor to the economy for many years, but an eventual decline in the world commodity market rendered its production unrewarding. Since the country's independence in 1975, there has been a dramatic drop in copra output and the number of people employed on coconut plantations. Palm oil has become the country's biggest agricultural product, thanks to its high yield. Large palm oil plantations and processing plants are in Oro, Milne Bay, and the western part of New Britain.

Although tea grown in the highlands is pleasant to drink, it has not met economic expectations and lags behind cocoa and copra as a potential revenue earner. Rubber production is growing slowly, and tobacco is a cash crop produced for the domestic market. Vanilla has become a significant export since the early 2000s and is one of a number of spices that are farmed for cash.

The flesh and seeds of palm oil fruit yield a yellow oil used as edible fat and for making items such as soap and candles.

HIGH-QUALITY HIGHLAND COFFEE

Coffee accounts for 18.5 percent of Papua New Guinea's agricultural exports and 4.7 percent of all export income. Most of it is cultivated in the five highland provinces of Simbu, Enga, Eastern Highlands, Western Highlands, and Southern Highlands. Up to 91 percent of the coffee is cultivated on small plots averaging slightly more than an acre (0.4 ha) in size, many of which are clan holdings. The mild arabica bean that predominates is of a high quality and much in demand, and there are about 80 coffee-processing facilities that prepare the beans for local consumption or export. Coffee beans that are ready for picking resemble bright red berries. After picking, the berries are placed in a concrete trough where the fleshy part is left to rot. The outer coats of the seeds are then dried and removed, and the remainder of the beans are collected.

ENVIRONMENT

UNLIKE MANY DEVELOPED NATIONS, which have both the wealth and the awareness to make environmental conservation a priority, Papua New Guinea is caught between needing to exploit its natural resources for income and needing to preserve the environment for future generations. Widespread environmental degradation from mining and forestry and associated problems such as pollution, erosion, and threats to unique species of plants and animals are some of the issues the country is grappling with. In addition, the lack of waste management and recycling facilities is increasingly a problem as the population expands.

Geographically isolated from Southeast Asia since the island of New Guinea separated from the supercontinent Gondwanaland millions of years ago, Papua New Guinea has an unusually high number of animal species that are unique to the country. Its diverse habitats are also home to an enormous number of plant species. The importance of this biodiversity is recognized internationally by scientists and by nongovernmental organizations that provide conservation programs that Papua New Guinea nationals themselves are unable to fund.

"Papua New Guinea is a cornucopia of ecology. It ranks within the top five most diverse countries in the world with an estimated 21,000 types of higher plants, 242 species of mammals, and 762 species of birds."

—Embassy of Papua New Guinea to the Americas

Left: **Beautiful aquatic reefs such as the one shown are in danger of being wiped out by pollution.**

Opposite: **Waterfalls pouring out from a cave and into a gorge in the middle of the forest. Papua New Guinea is home to some of the most beautiful and diverse rain forests in the world.**

These glaciers in Puncak Jaya in Indonesia are melting due to global warming. This will cause the water level in Papua New Guinea to rise, with ill effects on human and aquatic life.

EARLY SIGNS OF GLOBAL WARMING

Due to its limited manufacturing sector, Papua New Guinea uses few carbon fuels and generates only 0.45 tons (0.41 tonnes) of carbon dioxide emissions per person each year, compared with 22.5 tons (20.4 tonnes) per person in the United States. However, removal of forests is another source of greenhouse gases, causing roughly 20 percent of the world's heat-trapping gases each year. The rate of deforestation in Papua New Guinea is thought to account for an additional 32.1 tons (29.2 tonnes) of greenhouse emissions per person per year. These gases are believed to be adding to the warming effect in the earth's atmosphere, leading to widespread environmental change.

Until recently there was debate over whether global warming was really a threat. There is indeed evidence, however, that it is already affecting the environment of the island of New Guinea. In 2006, scientists visiting the Puncak Jaya area in the western central highlands of New Guinea, which is part of Indonesia, observed that the equatorial glacier there was melting at a rate that suggests the area is warming at twice the global rate, probably due to its altitude. This is likely to have significant effects on other high-altitude ecosystems across New Guinea, many of which are home to rare and even undiscovered species. Changes in rainfall, water levels, and temperature, and in turn in the vegetation, will alter the unique habitats that these animals rely upon, potentially endangering their existence.

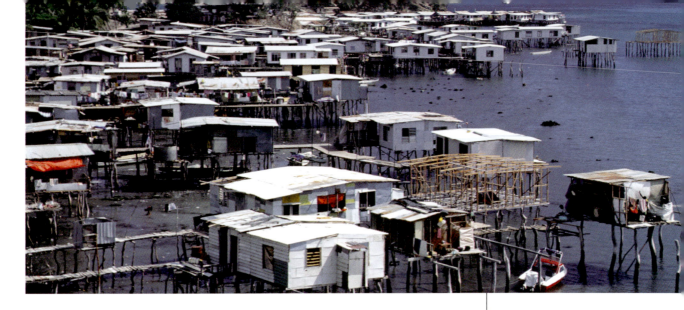

MINING POLLUTION

Mining has been a major source of income for Papua New Guinea for a century, but in recent decades huge open-cut mines have caused widespread environmental damage in remote areas. The construction of roads, mining camps, processing facilities, and the open-cut mines themselves disturb pristine wilderness areas, and the impact is usually felt for several miles around the mine sites.

The main problem in Papua New Guinea is that the mines don't use tailings dams—embankments to contain the waste products and excess fluid. Instead the mines discharge their crushed and chemically treated ore wastes directly into rivers and offshore waters. These "tailings" contain at least 50 percent sedimentation, as well as processing chemicals and other toxic substances such as heavy metals. These chemicals can poison aquatic species and gradually become more concentrated in the food chain, including traditional village foods. The effects are felt downstream all the way from the mine into coastal waters, where corals are particularly vulnerable to them. The Panguna mine in Bougainville, now closed, and the Ok Tedi mine in the Star Mountains in Western Province are two examples of the terrible impact this pollution has had in Papua New Guinea.

The government holds a large share of equity in the mines. Since it is both the environmental regulator and a part-owner, it sometimes relaxes conservation regulations in order to let the mining profits keep rolling in.

These houses built on stilts along the Port Moresby Bay are in danger of being submerged by the rising sea levels.

ENVIRONMENTAL DISASTER AT OK TEDI MINE

A tailings dam designed to remove tailings before releasing wastewater was originally planned for the Ok Tedi copper and gold mine in Western Province but was abandoned after an earthquake in 1984 revealed how geologically unstable the area was. The government subsequently allowed the mine to go ahead without the dam. An average of 90 million tons (91.44 billion kg) of waste and wastewater have been released into the Ok Tedi River and flowed downstream into the Fly River system each year since 1984, polluting them with arsenic and toxic heavy metals.

Ok Tedi Mining Limited reports that the water is of drinkable quality and aquatic life is not affected. Villagers downstream say that sago swamps and riverside gardens are dying and that the pigs and deer they hunt emit a terrible smell that makes them inedible. There are fewer fish, and those caught often have black metallic balls inside them from an accumulation of toxic waste metals. People have also experienced skin diseases and stomach problems from drinking the water. Meanwhile, flooding due to sedimentation has ruined houses and destroyed trees.

In 1994 and 2000, landowners filed lawsuits against BHP Billiton, which owned the major share in the mine. The company eventually settled out of court with a payment of $28.6 million and an agreement to dredge some parts of the river; it also sold off its interest in the mine. Some affected communities, however, have yet to receive any compensation or assistance. The mine is set to close in 2010.

FOREST LOSS

Logging is a significant source of income to Papua New Guinea, making up 4.8 percent of export earnings. Of the nation's 88,957,938 acres (36 million ha) of forest, 5,871,224 acres (2,376,000 ha), or 6.6 percent, have been logged between 1990 and 2005. Only 14,826,323–19,768,431 acres (6–8 million ha) remain of forest that is suitable for harvest in a sustainable manner; in other words, 20 percent of the commercially sustainable forest has already been logged. Some reports suggest that at this rate, Papua New Guinea could be completely logged out by as early as 2020. Foreign companies carried out most of the logging, and there have been problems with corruption in the granting of logging permits. Although the government developed tighter forestry regulations in the early 1990s aimed at creating sustainable practices, they are difficult to police in remote areas.

Commercial logging of klinkii pines is carried out by foreign companies. Once the valuable timber has been removed, the remainder is often burned to free the land for farming, which results in the loss of a great number of forests.

Forests are also cleared for farming and housing, particularly as the population grows and more land is needed for food crops. The use of fire to rapidly clear land sometimes causes widespread forest fires. Deforestation causes habitat damage, soil erosion and nutrient loss, pollution of waterways, and loss of wildlife corridors, which further endangers native animals and allows the introduction of invasive pest species into previously undisturbed areas. Removal of woodland can also limit traditional hunting and farming practices, leading to loss of culture. Along with old-growth forest loss, the logging operations themselves damage the wilderness areas, causing soil erosion along timber roads and camps and leading to the dumping of industrial and camp wastes and raw effluent. Logging operators are required to submit their plans for managing this waste, but in reality they are poorly monitored.

Ironically, new global interest in growing crops cheaply for the production of biofuel has placed increased pressure on forests in developing countries like Papua New Guinea. In January 2008 the Milne Bay government turned down plans to clear-cut 70 percent of Woodlark Island to make way for palm-oil plantations for biodiesel. The customary landowners fiercely opposed the plans. International conservation organizations supported their cause.

Woodlark Island is a good example of the biodiversity of the areas that are under threat from deforestation in Papua New Guinea. It is believed to have more than 20 endemic species of plant and animals, some so new they have not yet been named. A full wildlife survey of the island has yet to be taken. Widespread logging could decimate many of these species, possibly leading to their extinction.

EROSION AND SEDIMENTATION

Removal of vegetation coupled with high rainfall destabilizes soil and results in a high rate of erosion by wind and rain. Valuable nutrient-rich topsoil is washed away, leaving poorer, dustier, and drier soil behind. The silt ends up in watercourses, where it affects downstream ecosystems by blocking the light needed by algae and other water plants. It also alters the balance of nutrients in the water. This in turn harms some species of aquatic animals and has a flow-on effect in rivers, coastal floodplains, and marine waters, including coastal fish-hatchery areas. Because many communities rely on fishing and other food found in these environments, what starts as a bit of soil runoff can have widespread environmental and human impact downstream.

In 2005 the Papua New Guinea government announced 12 new protected forest, wetland, and reef areas, bringing the total area of protected land to 4 percent of the total landmass. The government has committed to protecting a total of 10 percent of the country by 2010.

VULNERABLE BIODIVERSITY

Between 5 and 7 percent of the world's total number of species are believed to be found in Papua New Guinea, with more than 20,000 species of flowering plants alone. A large number of native animals are found only in Papua New Guinea's uniquely diverse habitats. Twenty-four species were discovered as recently as 2005, and many of these are rare plants and animals that inhabit only small areas. Of the 214 known species of mammals in Papua New Guinea, more than a quarter are thought to be endangered.

Along with habitat loss due to logging, mining, and agriculture, more animals are being killed through traditional hunting and fishing as the population swells. Among the critically endangered species are a number of sawfish, the leatherback and hawksbill turtles, three types of bat, two species of water rats, and two types of mice. Four of these are endemic, including the Bulmer's fruit bat, which was first described from 12,000-year-old fossils and only discovered alive in 1975. Other endangered mammals include the Alpine wallaby, the Fergusson Island striped possum, the Goodfellow's Tree-kangaroo, the long-beaked echidna, and the Poncelet's giant rat.

The Goodfellow's Tree-kangaroo will be in danger if the forests in Papua New Guinea are dramatically reduced.

About 52 species of endangered animals have been declared national animals by the Papua New Guinea government. National animals are protected by law and can be killed only in the traditional manner for customary uses but cannot be bought, sold, kept, or exported. They include all 33 types of birds of paradise as well as several other types of birds, all seven species of birdwing butterflies, the long-beaked echidna, the dugong, and the Boelen's python.

Children running through the mountain of waste surrounding their home.

WASTE MANAGEMENT

In traditional life, everything that the villagers used was sourced from their surroundings and could safely be discarded back into the environment, burned, or left to rot in a pile. These practices do not work with modern nonbiodegradable materials such as food packaging, however, and waste management remains an issue in Papua New Guinea. In large urban areas, contractors remove unsorted household and industrial waste to landfill dumps, where they are haphazardly burned or buried. Some householders burn or bury their own garbage, while others leave it in piles.

A certain amount of de facto recycling—sale or reuse of discarded items such as clothes, building materials, furniture, and household goods—takes place in areas where cash is scarce. There are commercial scrap-metal recyclers in the urban centers, and people collect aluminum cans and glass bottles for the small fee that these companies pay. Recycling does not extend to paper or plastics, and plastic waste is problematic. Plastic bags and packaging are commonly discarded, often finding their way into waterways, or are burned, releasing toxic gases.

The country struggles with agricultural wastes arising from the processing of plantation crops such as palm oil and coffee. The by-products from these are routinely released into waterways, where they strip the water of oxygen necessary for aquatic life. The good news is that these by-products are increasingly being diluted and used effectively for irrigation on palm-oil plantations. However, because more than half of the country's coffee is grown by smallholders who do not have the resources for treatment, much of the coffee waste is dumped raw, and the water in these areas is unfit for drinking.

CONSERVATION MOVEMENT

The government of Papua New Guinea committed the country to the principles of conservation and environmental sustainability when it ratified the United Nations Convention on Biological Diversity in 1993. The Department of Environment and Conservation is responsible for protecting Papua New Guinea's natural resources, and it administers legislation covering national parks, protection and controlled farming of fauna, environmental planning, regulation of hazardous materials, and management of water resources.

The bulk of conservation work, however, is done by nongovernmental organizations, most of which are internationally funded. They work primarily with small groups of local people to create awareness of environmental issues and to teach people how to preserve their local resources by using ecologically sound practices and developing sustainable sources of income, such as village-based logging using portable sawmills referred to as "wokabaut" sawmills, ecotourism, insect farming, sustainable deep-water fishing, artifact production, and small-scale organic crops. They are also politically and legally active, lobbying to stop further destruction of the environment, particularly by large mining and logging companies.

Greenpeace members in the UK demonstrating against the use of illegally logged timber from the rain forests of Papua New Guinea. In addition to the Papua New Guinea locals, international organizations are concerned with the loss of important ecosystems in Papua New Guinea.

PAPUA NEW GUINEANS

THE PHYSICAL FEATURES OF PEOPLE IN Papua New Guinea vary greatly in terms of skin coloring, facial structure, and even body size. Most people have mixed racial origins—Papuan, Melanesian, Micronesian, and Polynesian. Papuans and Melanesians, who make up 95 percent of the population, are believed to be related to the Ainoids, people with a heavy brow line who are thought to be the ancestors of the Australian aborigines. Micronesians and Polynesians are related to the Mongoloid race. The demarcations between groups are indeterminate, and clan ties are more important than racial distinctions. It is common for a person to identify with a clan or tribal name—for example, Motu or Duna. On the basis of cultural and historical connections, regional groupings have developed as follows: New Guineans (northern mainland), Papuans (southern mainland), highlanders, and islanders.

Left: **The traditional protection in rainy weather is a large hood made from bark, bark cloth, or simply a large banana leaf held over the head.**

Opposite: **Simbu women form a circle at the start of a pig slaughtering dance.**

POPULATION AND CHANGES

In 2007 the population was estimated to be 6.33 million people, but it is growing so quickly that it is conservatively estimated to exceed 7.3 million by the year 2015. This sudden rise indicates improved national health conditions and the lack of a widespread use of birth control. The rapid population explosion is expected to exert enormous pressure on health and education services, housing, and national resources.

The country has a young population, with 39.9 percent under the age of 15, and 68 percent under the age of 30. The life expectancy remains low at 53.7 years for males and 54.8 years for females. The average birthrate is quite high, at 4.1 births for each childbearing woman.

The death rate stands at 10.7 deaths per 1,000 people; the world average is nine deaths per 1,000. While development has brought improved medicine and modern technologies, it has also resulted in the gradual erosion of a traditional lifestyle. People are no longer driven to observe taboos that formerly had a stabilizing effect, and gambling and excessive alcohol consumption have caused financial and social hardship to many. The challenge for the population today seems to be to discover what is truly valuable to them and to use this as a guideline to steer their lives.

WANTOK: *FAMILY, CLAN, AND TRIBE*

Family, clan, and tribe are the essential social units. Of these, the extended family network is the most influential, and an intricate system of personal responsibilities and family obligations dictates the behavior

Women and children with branches for firewood.

of an individual in any given situation. A household may be called on to share its food, home, labor, land, or pigs with a family member or someone from the same tribe, whether the relation is close or distant. This is in accordance with the Melanesian concept of *wantok* (WAN-tohk), which acts as a social security network. A system of reciprocity means that something will usually be given in return—perhaps loyalty in a time of conflict or help at a later date.

Property, a prerequisite of wealth, does not always belong to the individual here in the way that it does to Westerners. In some instances land and jewelry are owned by the whole clan or tribe and distributed according to a complex network of ties. Ownership is often vested in the household, which is usually headed by a male. Wealth is determined not just by the things one has but also in the measure that one gives them away to others.

The village elders, or "big men," are often required to display their affluence by giving wealth away. This in return provides them with a great deal of influence because the villagers are then indebted to them. Big men do the heavy negotiating, settle disputes, and plan when to slaughter the pigs. An elaborate system of negotiation, trading ceremonies, and ritualized battles exists among clans throughout the country to preserve or restore order.

A Huli man in a distinctive wig made from human hair and held together with woven string. The women of the tribe do most of the work while the men concentrate on displaying their finery.

SELF-ADORNMENT

Western-style clothes are common in the urban areas and are being adopted increasingly in rural areas, particularly around Christian missions. They tend to be casual and geared toward the tropical climate. The women wear simple dresses or skirts and blouses, while the men wear shorts with a shirt, though in the rural areas the shirts are dispensable. Traditional clothing remains the norm for some tribes in the more remote areas, where Western-style clothing is not accessible, and it is commonly worn for special events throughout the country.

The intimate relationship that the various clans share with their environment is evident in the vibrant hues and ornate clothes they wear, both at ceremonies and daily. Feathers, bones, leaves, seeds, shells, and natural pigments are the basis for dress. Often such finery has symbolic meanings—it represents the qualities of the wearer or the individual's status or is a symbol of myths and customs revered by the tribe.

In Papua New Guinea, the native clothes are adorned with decorations, and often they are veritable works of art. The bright plumage of birds of paradise and other types of feathers are woven into elaborate headdresses for the men. These are then decorated with valuable shells and animal teeth. Several groups, such as the Huli and the Komblo in the highlands, weave huge wigs from human hair and burrs, then decorate them with paints, dried flowers, and even iridescent beetles. The highlanders in particular favor nose piercing. The septum, the fleshy wall between the two nostrils, is pierced with a sharp piece of wood, bone, or cassowary quill, and any variety of impressive objects are placed through the hole, including boar tusks, cassowary quills or bones, long dried grasses, or shells.

Loincloths, or *laplaps* (LAP-laps), tend to resemble aprons, with a longer section of cloth or strands of woven cords and leaves worn at the front and a smaller bunch of leaves tucked into the waistband behind. Males of several tribes near the western border wear penis gourds and little else. The gourds are long marrowlike fruit, up to 3 feet (0.9 meters) in length. These are dried, cut open and worn over the penis and tied to the waist with string. Cassowary bones, daggers, and tools are tucked into woven armbands and leg bands. Sometimes ritual scar designs are cut into the flesh at a boy's coming-of-age ceremony, especially among those living along the Sepik River, where the designs represent the claw marks of crocodiles.

The painting of faces, bodies, and hair is practiced by both genders, traditionally with charcoal and pigments, though modern paints are now favored, especially for ceremonies, for their brightness. In some areas, both men and women rub their skins with a variety of leaves and oils, including pig fat, to leave an attractive sheen.

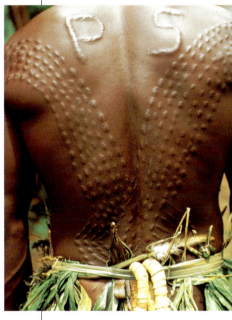

Ritual scar designs are cut into the flesh over the arms, shoulders, and upper body. Clay and ashes are rubbed into the cuts to ensure that they heal as raised keloid scars.

WOMEN'S DRESSING

Women's traditional dress is colorful but less elaborate than the men's. It is customary in some areas for women to wear tattoos on the face. The tattoos are made in a painful process, using just a needle and charcoal. Lines of dots in the shapes of suns, stars, and arrows, as well as curved parallel lines, decorate the face.

Women in most areas traditionally wear plain grass or other simple skirts and are sometimes bare breasted. In some regions, unwed girls modestly cover themselves with a small woven patch of fabric. Strings of beads, leaves, feathers, and teeth are worn in abundance during ceremonial occasions.

While women wear headdresses for special events, these tend to be smaller and less ornate than those of the men. Huge woven bags called *bilums* (BILL-uhms), made of bark fiber or nylon, are used to carry everything from babies to firewood, with the strap placed on the head to support the weight of the load falling behind.

WOMEN IN MOURNING

In several areas, women in mourning wear numerous loops of grass seeds that range in color from pale gray to white. These are referred to in English as Job's tears. A full load of these can weigh up to 31 pounds (14 kg). Each day the woman removes one loop. Mourning ends when she takes off the last loop of seeds, which is usually about nine months after the death of her husband. In some areas, the women coat themselves with a bluish gray clay while in mourning.

Among the Dani in West Papua, it is customary for the widow and other close female relatives of the dead man to have part of a finger removed from above the first joint as part of the funeral. The finger-cutting ceremony is seen as a way of expressing grief and placating the ancestral spirits. A male member of the tribe who performs the ritual knocks the grieving woman's elbow sharply on a stone to numb the arm before he uses a small stone adze to sever the finger. The remaining stump is wrapped in healing plants, and the hand is bound in a banana leaf.

The men conduct virtually all negotiations and village politics. Nevertheless, a woman is sometimes forced by circumstances to take on a man's duties if he is hunting or seeking paid employment away from the village.

POWERFUL TABOOS

Just as the men in a clan have their secret rituals, the women in some Papua New Guinean communities have secret knowledge, which is never passed on to the men, involving magic and traditional medicine. The fear of being cursed by a witch holds many a brave hunter in its grip. There are powerful taboos relating to menstruation, the effects of which are believed to be so potent that in some tribes all the women sleep in a separate dwelling away from the other villagers.

In certain places along the Sepik the women even have their own separate walking tracks in the village. In some areas the men cook their own food believing that any contact with women would weaken them. Men often protect themselves with herbs and magic before engaging in sexual relations with their wives. In the Sepik area, the men often wile away their day lounging around in the cool shade of the men's houses, which the women are barred from entering.

LIFESTYLE

THE PEOPLE IN THE URBAN AREAS AND THE RURAL AREAS live vastly different lifestyles. The urban areas provide the comforts of modern living, with Western-style housing, shopping, and conveniences. The remote villages, on the other hand, rarely have electricity, unless cash crops or mining has bought in some wealth and electricity generators. They also lack proper roads and sanitary water supplies. Swarms of mosquitoes and sand flies fill the air near any swamp or watercourse, and the smoke-filled interiors of houses are the only deterrent to these pests.

Only 13 percent of the population live in the urban centers, with the rest living in the rural areas. The government provides some funding for low-cost housing, particularly in Port Moresby and Lae, but demand always exceeds supply. As a result, people construct small dwellings using an assortment of materials. These shelters are often clustered at the urban fringes and soon develop into shantytowns.

Left: **People are drawn to the cities like Mount Hagen in search of work and material gain, and the country is witnessing a growing cash economy.**

Opposite: **Girls from the Trobriand Islands are bringing yams back home after the harvest.**

Many houses are constructed on stilts as protection against flooding and to facilitate defense in times of fighting; the stilts also position the houses above the height at which many mosquitoes and sand flies swarm.

VILLAGE LIFE

Outside the towns, most housing is constructed using the resources found in the forests or the swamps, with the occasional addition of industrial materials such as corrugated iron sheets. The structures vary from small huts at ground level—with a single room housing an entire family—to large communal longhouses accommodating an extended family or segregated groups of men and women.

The houses are arranged in long rows or in circular clusters and may be rectangular or round. The house frame is a strong wooden or bamboo structure, and it is topped with thatched roofs of strong kunai grass, sago palm fronds, or other broad leaves. Wooden or bamboo slats or bark laced together with thin cane strips form the walls. In many areas houses are built on stilts.

A fire is usually left smoldering in a central hearth of dirt or stones or in a clay fire bowl. People like to sit around the fire mainly because the smoke helps to keep away mosquitoes. After dark the fire is often the only source of light in villages with little or limited access to electricity or gas. The smoke escapes through any exit it can, as windows are not necessarily desirable in a land that is infested with flying insects, drenched in monsoonal rains, and susceptible to tribal warfare. Inside the house there may be wooden beds, mats, or coarse fiber bedcovers. Food and other goods are commonly stored in baskets or string bags hung from the rafters or in unglazed clay pots.

A village clearing is reserved for communal gatherings, and it is typically the women's job to sweep it. Many highland villages have a wide ditch built around them to protect them against attacks and to prevent pigs, chickens, and small children from wandering out into the surrounding wilderness.

WEALTH IN SHELLS AND PIGS

Paper money and coins are relatively new in Papua New Guinea. Paper money was particularly mistrusted. As recently as 30 years ago, some people insisted on being paid only in coins. Even today many people attach more value to traditional wealth than to the national currency. While a large pig may be worth 500–1,000 kina, many people would prefer to own the pig itself instead of the cash. Likewise, cassowaries and any weapons or jewelry made from parts of this animal are highly sought after.

The national currency is named after the kina shell, a large crescent shape cut from the gold-lipped pearl shell. Kina shells are worn proudly on a length of string threaded between two holes in the shell and are still used in trade and barter. Occasionally an individual shell will be given its own name, and the number of knots in its string indicates the number of owners the shell has had. In the highlands it is common to see long necklaces made of tiny bamboo sticks strung in a ladderlike fashion. Each strip on these *omak* (OH-mak) necklaces represents either 10 pigs or 10 kina shells given away or lent by the owner, an important indication of the wearer's social status.

Trade is commonly conducted with nonpaper money. In Milne Bay, business can be conducted with grass skirts or dry bundles of etched banana leaves called *doba* (DOH-bah) for yams and shell valuables. In New Britain, *tambu* (TAHM-boo), tiny shells strung on a piece of bamboo, are used as currency, especially in the markets.

Currency still in use includes kina shells. Like the kina shell after which it is named, the one-kina coin has a hole in the middle so that it can be strung and worn around the neck.

A Japanese-made mini-truck serving as a PMV, or public motor vehicle. Each PMV has a government-employed driver and a conductor who finds out where one intends to disembark and collects the fare midway through any trip.

MOVING AROUND

The fastest and easiest way to travel in Papua New Guinea is by air. Much of the country's development has depended on its aviation facilities, and most mineral and forestry exploration takes place with sophisticated equipment transported by air. Many of the airstrips are small and rough, however, and flights often have long waiting lists.

Along the waterways, especially the Sepik River, the dugout canoe is king. The traffic can get quite heavy on the river on market days. Large and midsize freighters and passenger boats provide transportation between the islands, but it may take a couple of days to reach a destination because freight is loaded on or taken off along the way. Villagers make use of their own boats, which include traditional canoes, diesel-run wooden boats, and small dinghies with outboard motors known as speedies or banana boats.

The majority of roads are rough, and travelers can be ambushed by armed robbers. Sometimes heavy rainfall converts roads into impassable muddy bogs. Nevertheless, they are useful for shorter journeys and for those with little money. One can choose to walk, the road often being the only clearing through dense vegetation, or to take a PMV—a public motor vehicle. A PMV can be just about any vehicle, from a truck with hard benches to a Japanese-made minibus. PMVs travel along predetermined routes through the towns and the countryside. Despite a lack of policing of the roads in the rural areas, the PMVs are quite safe to travel in because the drivers are aware of the stiff fines should they run over even a chicken, let alone if they injure a pedestrian or a passenger.

LAND TENURE

About 97 percent of land in Papua New Guinea comes under traditional landownership laws, a stark contrast to the Western system based on individual ownership backed by legal documents. Traditional ownership is based on human memory, often held by a community, and is distributed according to a complex web of individual and clan rights. The systems differ from place to place. Disputes between tribes over landownership boundaries are a historical cause of warfare, and tensions can still run high today between groups and clans within any single tribe.

Some areas remain communally owned. This becomes a problem when land transfer is required for nontraditional purposes—for example, the sale of land for cash cropping or the establishment of mining rights in a particular area. Different groups may stake their claim on a single piece of land based on each group's oral history, and disputes inevitably arise. Sometimes the wrong group of people is paid compensation for the use of the land.

Pieces of land such as this are constantly being fought over by various groups of people. Some government road- and electricity- projects as well as proposed mining developments may cross several traditional boundaries. A situation then arises in which too many groups claim compensation and the project has to be abandoned because of mounting costs.

71

The men of a certain tribe parading through their land. Payback must be made for deaths incurred in battle. If a village is unable to make the payment immediately, a truce is declared for the duration of the payback term, which can last for months or even years.

PAYBACK AND WARFARE

In Papua New Guinea, everything is owned by someone. Even seemingly remote areas of land have a traditional owner somewhere, and the ownership of individual animals is known throughout the entire village. If land is to be used, the owners expect immediate and generous compensation or rent. Any damage, whether intended or accidental, to life, limb, or property requires ritual compensation to avert similar violence in return.

The size of tribal communities varies from a few hundred to a few thousand members, and there are often traditional intertribal hostilities. Each tribe or clan is collectively held responsible for the actions of its individual members and actively seeks compensation if one of its members becomes a victim. Failing to make the appropriate payback compensation is a worse crime than the original act, and revenge is accordingly brutal. Pigs are the favored payback currency, although other goods such as kina shells, food items, cash, and even cartons of beer are acceptable. Tribal war may result when negotiations between clans or tribes fail.

BORROWING FROM THE CLAN

The bride price asked is usually more than what the hopeful man can afford, and he ends up borrowing heavily from his clan. This obligates him to the clan and draws him closer into its complex structure. The entire amount goes to the bride's parents and clan, and the new couple receives none of it. The bride price encourages the bride's parents to prepare her for the duties of marriage. In some communities, if the marriage breaks down or if the wife is sent back to her family, the bride price must be returned in full, along with interest on the price.

BRIDE PRICE AS MARRIAGE CONTRACT

Marriage is less about the individual's ties and more about the wider social relationships that are strengthened through the marriage contract. An essential element is the payment of a "bride price" by the groom to his bride's parents or clan.

The traditional marriage ceremony in many areas of Papua New Guinea centers on the final payment of the bride price. The groom and his clan, dressed in their customary finery, walk to the ceremonial clearing where the goods are laid out in front of the bride's clan. Leaf-wrapped kina shells rubbed with red ocher, pigs, cash notes attached to a large display pole, and even cassowaries can form part of this important payment. They are examined by the bride's family, and once the goods are accepted the marriage is sealed.

These payments are still common even in the cities, where marriages take place between members of clans from different provinces, and among Christians too, who are married with a church ceremony. Despite efforts by village councils to control the prices, payments can be high. In the highlands they can consist of scores of pigs and a small cash payment. In the cities thousands of kina can change hands, and the sum can rise even higher among wealthy families.

In the Mendi region, brides are dressed in black for their weddings and are required to wear this for an entire month afterward. They darken their skin with soot and tigaso oil, which is also black.

Traditionally adultery was considered a crime worse than murder. It was seen as an insult to the aggrieved spouse's entire clan and was punishable by death. Today this strict code has been relaxed, but adultery is still a very serious offense in some groups.

Childbirth is a risk. The infant mortality rate is high, and in some areas a child is not named for up to 12 months after he is born because it is believed that if he dies with a given name, his spirit would need attention. Maternal mortality is high too, with more than three maternal deaths for every 1,000 births.

A woman selling her woven textiles in a market. When the country gained its independence, the government named one of its goals "a rapid increase in the equal and active participation of women in all forms of economic and social activity."

THE ROLE OF WOMEN

Women are traditionally considered subordinate to men, although there are exceptions. In a few societies in the New Guinea islands and Milne Bay, property is passed on matrilineally—that is, men inherit property through the female line. For example, a man may inherit goods from his mother's brother. After all, women in these societies perform the bulk of the subsistence farming, tend pigs, raise children, and prepare food.

Nevertheless, the women are not accorded social or political equality. The men are still custodians of family property, wield power in decision-making, and receive the cash and the choicest cuts of food. The women have little recourse should they disagree with their husbands, fathers, or elders. Many men feel justified in beating their wives or daughters. While this is illegal, the law fails to protect women, because it is virtually impossible to report such cases to the police, especially in the remote areas.

There are instances when the women band together to form groups and collectives. They have also set up their own trading networks, shareholding concerns, and educational support systems. This way they are achieving success and reaping monetary and social benefits. Some women have risen above the obstacles placed before them to reach management level in both private and public sectors or respected positions in their home communities.

Paid employment seems the best opportunity to leave behind the traditional requirement of subservience, as it allows the women to participate in a modern world. The difficulty is that many rural societies still hold negative perceptions about sending their daughters to school. The labor a girl provides in tending to her domestic chores is much greater than that of her brother, so in times of financial crisis the girl is taken out of school before her brother.

Men often regard a woman's value as they would a commodity. Because the women are responsible for agricultural production, having a wife is a requirement for adding to one's wealth. In some areas, the amount of land allotted to a man's family for farming depends on the number of women he has in the household, and polygamy is practiced in many areas to maximize wealth and status. In the highlands the more wives a man has, the more pigs they can rear for him. "Big men" in particular have several wives, who are regarded as a symbol of prestige. Daughters who marry earn their parents a bride payment that can be quite substantial. The parents may be tempted to choose the union that is most profitable or politically beneficial to themselves ahead of their daughter's needs.

A female cashier serves a customer at a Western-style supermarket.

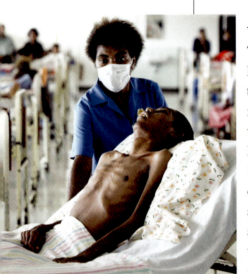

A nurse taking care of a dying HIV patient in Port Moresby's General Hospital.

HEALTH CARE

The health system is deteriorating as the population grows, and life expectancy figures are still low. Health services are delivered through a system of small first-aid posts staffed by orderlies with rudimentary medical and hygiene skills and larger health centers with a higher level of expertise. There are also 19 provincial hospitals with trained medical staff. On average there are 13 doctors to attend to every 100,000 people, but most of these doctors work in Port Moresby. The Christian churches provide around 60 percent of health services in rural areas. They run several hospitals and train many nurses and all community health workers. In many areas people still administer their own healing methods, ranging from medicinal plants to body paint.

Malaria is endemic along the coast and along with pneumonia accounts for a third of all recorded deaths. Wide-scale mobile vaccination programs have halted the spread of infectious diseases such as measles and yaws, a highly contagious skin disease. Climate and remoteness hamper large-scale health improvements, however, and tuberculosis is on the rise again. An HIV/AIDS epidemic was declared in 2003, with 2 percent of all people aged 15–49 believed to have contracted the disease. Current estimates are that 64,000 people are HIV-positive or have AIDS.

Malnutrition is a factor in many deaths, because people with a weakened immune system do not respond well to treatment for even simple illnesses. About 39 percent of the population has access to safe drinking water, but many people do not understand the relationship between poor sanitation and disease, and diarrheal diseases remain common. Education about hygiene and nutrition is needed in all regions for the standard of health to improve.

EDUCATION

The national literacy rate has improved rapidly, with 57.3 percent of the adult population able to read. When Papua New Guinea gained its independence, the government expressed two goals concerning education: universal education at the primary level and access to higher education for as many as possible.

The first six years of education, starting at the age of seven, are compulsory, with classes held in government-provided, community-based schools. In remote areas, these schools are sometimes open-air, palm-thatched structures, and having them around does not guarantee enrollment. Most instruction takes place in English and in pidgin, although 7 percent of children in elementary schools learn to read and write in Tok Ples, the local language, until grade three, when English instruction begins.

For higher education, there is the University of Papua New Guinea in Port Moresby, the University of Technology in Lae, the University of Goroka, and the University of Vudal. There are also two smaller Christian universities, along with colleges of technical and vocational education, such as teaching and nursing, in most provinces.

A teachers' training college in Goroka teaches silk screening as a craft in addition to the usual academic learning.

RELIGION

THERE SEEM TO BE AS MANY BELIEF SYSTEMS in Papua New Guinea as there are tribes and languages. For thousands of years, communities isolated from each other passed on their unique myths and rituals, most of them based on people's close contact with their surrounding landscape. The presence of a forest or a river is keenly felt and respected, for although it provides sustenance, it can also sometimes be a cruel adversary to human existence.

Two elements are common in the traditional beliefs of Papua New Guineans: the practice of magic and the belief in a spirit world. Some spirits are regarded as belonging to the recently dead and to ancestors, with other types of spirits inhabiting the natural world as well.

Christianity is the professed religion of about 96 percent of Papuan nationals. There are also small Baha'i, Buddhist, and Muslim communities in Papua New Guinea.

Spirits may be malevolent and therefore require placating. Less malevolent spirits are sometimes courted, and important ventures are never started without first seeking the spirits' approval and intervention.

Left: **Tribal men carrying their traditional poles. Many old beliefs revolve around superstition and fear of the unknown.**

Opposite: **In a blend of traditional customs meeting modern ideologies, this spirit house used to be a sacred meeting house for tribe members but has now been converted into a church.**

A Christian baptism by water immersion in a lake.

CHRISTIAN CHURCHES

Christianity was introduced early in the country's history during contact between the local people and the outside world. Missions were set up throughout the country by Christians who spent decades living close to and working with the local people. The influence of the various churches was such that by 1960, Papua New Guinea had become a predominantly Christian country. Even today churches continue to run and fund hospitals, plantations, and schools.

Although approximately 96 percent of the population identify themselves as Christians, many do not participate in church activities on a regular basis. The major Christian churches and organizations represented are Roman Catholic, Lutheran, United Church, Seventh-day Adventist, Anglican, Baptist, and Pentecostal, along with the Evangelical Church Alliance and the Salvation Army. Many who profess a belief in Christianity practice clan rituals as well as attend church without experiencing any apparent conflict of ideals.

CANNIBALISM

Papua New Guinea's laws support the right of the individual to practice his or her beliefs freely, provided those beliefs do not infringe on the general principles of humanity. One practice that the colonial government outlawed almost immediately upon discovering it was cannibalism. Cannibalism, or the eating of human flesh, was practiced for centuries by groups such as the Hewa and the Fore. It is not about murder; those who eat the flesh of their fellow clan members who have died from natural causes or disease do so because they believe that it protects them from illness or to release the spirit of the deceased from the body. These groups believe that a spirit that is not released is doomed to spend its days in a sort of limbo.

The body was prepared and cooked by a strict code, then divided among clan members according to each individual's relationship to the deceased. At one time it was considered an honor to partake in this practice. Hostility toward the *guvmen* (GUV-men), or government, which declared this practice illegal, caused the Hewa region in the southern highlands to be closed to outsiders until 1965.

Some head-hunting tribes had the custom of bleaching the skulls of their victims and putting them on display in their villages as trophies. These skulls were a testament to the clan's prowess and the might of their ancestors.

FATAL LAUGHING DISEASE

Cannibalistic feasting on the bodies of deceased relatives seems to have resulted in the transmission of disease rather than its prevention. *Kuru* is an agonizing and fatal "laughing disease" that affects the central nervous system. More women than men have contracted this disease, probably because the men were greatly restricted by taboos concerning the body parts they were allowed to consume.

The link between *kuru* and cannibalistic practices was discovered by a Christian mission. However, the locals continued to attribute the disease to sorcery and remained unconvinced for a long time that cannibalism was harmful. It is believed that cannibalism is no longer practiced, and while a few people continue to fall ill with *kuru*, it is thought to be the result of the long incubation period of the disease.

The roof of a spirit house in the Sepik region of Papua New Guinea.

PLACES OF WORSHIP

Christian churches and mission houses are present throughout Papua New Guinea and vary widely in design and complexity. Urban centers tend to have larger churches constructed in a modern Western manner, while in rural areas they can be simple halls made from whatever local materials are available.

Outside the influence of Christianity, traditional beliefs are still followed. Along the middle Sepik are soaring *haus tambarans* (house TAM-bor-ans), or spirit houses, in which items of cultural and religious significance are stored. They are made from materials similar to those used in the local houses but have high prowlike facades. These have decorative panels carved and painted with ancestral faces in the form of masks or representations of spirit animals or totems. Initiated and about-to-be initated men are the only ones permitted to enter these houses, and it is believed that a breach of this taboo can result in death to the offender. Fertility rites, magical ceremonies, and male initiations take place here.

The other important religious space is the clearing in the village, where all types of dances, singing, and communal rituals take place. The rituals enact traditional stories and beliefs, prepare people for important events, or try to bring about a desired outcome. Taboos and traditions dictate the form and proceedings of these rituals, including the costumes and the body paint used, the words sung, the music played, the people who participate, and even the food consumed.

MAGIC AND SORCERY

A feature of Melanesian society is widespread belief in magic, practiced by ordinary people for beneficial reasons (for example, to aid healing) and by sorcerers who wield it for power. The magic practiced by the ordinary people through their superstitions and daily rituals permeates all areas of village life. The magic of sorcerers, on the other hand, is veiled in secrecy and fear, and disease and misfortune are attributed to the workings of enemy sorcerers. In some societies, women use the men's fear of their witchcraft to manipulate them.

Within many communities, magic is still practiced daily to ensure successful harvests, gain victory over a warring tribe, or find a suitable mate. Plants are cultivated or gathered for these purposes, as well as for use as medicine, and their application is accompanied by rituals and spells.

Some tribes seek revenge against those who have wronged them by bringing illness on their enemies. Sometimes magic is invoked to cast illness on an entire clan or tribe. At other times, the sorcerer seeks to replace an individual victim's spirit with a stone, causing the person to die. It is also believed that sickness can be inflicted by collecting a victim's personal items and knotting them in a special way. Burning the whole parcel could result in death.

A shaman of the Huli tribe poses by a sacred altar with painted skulls.

A bird mask represents the people's belief in the spirit world.

SPIRIT ANIMALS

The most important spirits are usually those of ancestors, but in some areas nonhuman spirits feature more prominently. These may be perceived in animal or monster forms. For example, people living near the Sepik fear the crocodile *masalai* (mass-ah-LAY), or spirit, and offerings of *buai* (bwai), or betel nut, are thrown into treacherous rapids inhabited by the *masalai*. Such spirits are believed to have individual personalities and to be able to communicate their anger or goodwill. People take great care to please the spirits, believing that they can affect the fortune of an individual or a tribe, and this forms an integral part of ritualistic beliefs and practices.

Birds play a significant role in these traditions. Each Dani clan has ties with a particular bird species, which is considered to be a clan member. To the Enga, who live in the western highlands, different bird species are inhabited by ghosts, and hearing their call requires certain behaviors to avert personal disaster or to prevent the ghosts from attacking.

Not all spirit animals are considered evil. Some spirits are thought to bring about bountiful crops, successful hunting, and personal achievement.

Beliefs regarding spirit animals are slowly being transformed as Christianity spreads, education reaches more people, and the skeptical ways of the modern world take on a greater influence.

SONG, DANCE, AND FIRESIDE STORIES

Singing and dancing are not only an outlet for entertainment but also important methods of handing down oral histories to succeeding generations. They provide a valuable means of committing information to the communal memory in the absence of written records. Songs are composed for important events such as initiations and funerals and to commemorate victories.

These songs and dances are sung or performed at festivals and ceremonies, but they are a part of daily life as well. During the planting of crops or the construction of houses, for example, both the men and the women sing, by themselves or in unison. In the highlands, a single voice sometimes rings out down the green hillside, followed by the response of chanting voices of all ages from nearby areas.

On some evenings, people gather around the fireside to sing and dance. This is often accompanied by storytelling. The storyteller is treated with great respect, and many tales deal with the existence of good and evil, the origin of special foods, family ties, warfare, the beginning of humankind, how people came to inhabit their special region, and the origin of the tribe or the clan. Such evenings are also the time to discuss day-to-day events and exchange news. Often the dividing lines between magic, religious beliefs, clan histories, and social ceremonies are difficult to distinguish. Many of the people's festivals and art are an expression of their religious beliefs.

The need to placate the spirits of their ancestors and the fear of evil influences are common themes in the stories of Papua New Guineans.

CREATION STORY

One story tells of a being that created humanity by drawing people in the sand, then pouring blood over them. The Mangen and Mamusi highlanders ascribe creation to Nutu, who created humans and placed their soul, or *kanu* (KAH-noo), inside their liver, or *lona* (LOH-na). In death, the *kanu* flies back to Nutu, who is the master of all things.

LANGUAGE

MORE THAN 700 LANGUAGES AND DIALECTS are spoken in Papua New Guinea. Some languages are spoken by only a few hundred people in a community, and neighboring villages only six miles (10 km) apart may have completely different languages. Enga, the indigenous language group with the largest number of speakers, is spoken by only about 165,000 people. While some of the languages are related and share common dialects, many are radically different in origin. They are generally classified as either Austronesian or non-Austronesian.

Austronesian languages include those spoken in Indonesia and the Philippines. Motu, spoken in the Port Moresby area, is an Austronesian language. The non-Austronesian languages, which are believed to be older, include those spoken in the highlands and in small areas on Bougainville, New Ireland, and New Britain. They defy simple classification.

Left: **An Australian teacher shows a deaf girl how to speak by feeling the sound of her voice through the vocal chords and then imitating the throat movement.**

Opposite: **A man leans against a wall while reading an English-language newspaper.**

Village children learning English on a chalkboard.

ENGLISH AS THE OFFICIAL LANGUAGE

When the country came under Australian governance, English was used in administration and education, and it was subsequently adopted as the official language of Papua New Guinea because of its commercial utility. Today it is the language of government, education, commerce, and higher levels of administration but is not yet spoken on a national scale. For now it is spoken by only the small percentage of the population who have access to formal education.

The government would like to encourage the use of English more widely, because teaching children in Tok Pisin, a pidgin language, means that a large number of school and technical books would have to be translated from English.

CREOLES

Hiri Motu, a language developed by the Motu for their trading expeditions in the Gulf of Papua and thus used outside its original borders, was adapted by the Armed Native Constabulary to become Police Motu in British New Guinea. It became a sort of lingua franca for people in the region until the introduction of English.

Difficulties in communication remained, however, and in the absence of a common language that would be easy for speakers of many tongues to adopt, a pidgin, Tok Pisin, developed in the late 19th century to fill the gap.

Tok Pisin is a mixture of English, German, and Melanesian words set within a Malay grammar pattern that is uncomplicated and easy to pick up. It is sometimes called Neo-Melanesian or Melanesian Pidgin, Papua New Guinea Pidgin, or Tok Boi. The language arose among the Melanesian people who were hired as plantation labor in Australia and the Pacific. Because it originated around Rabaul, the Melanesian contribution is strongly flavored by the language patterns found throughout the eastern part of New Britain. Other regions of the Pacific have their own pidgins.

Some of the words, especially the verbs, have a strong German origin, but Tok Pisin is based heavily on English, and this influence is increasingly felt. For example, a towel used to be called *laplap bilong waswas* (LAP-lap BEE-long WAS-was), or "cloth for washing," but is now referred to simply as *taul* (TAH-ol). Other words from geographically close languages such as Indonesian have crept in, and many modern Australian colloquialisms have been integrated into the vocabulary, making for colorful speech. *Naiswan* (NAIS-wan), for instance, comes from the Australian "nice one" and is used, as in Australia, to express congratulations or approval.

Tok Pisin has been criticized for being merely a crude, patronizing, and inferior version of English. In reality it is a highly effective language that is living and growing and has evolved some of its own features. Its

COUNTING IN TOK PISIN

Cardinal numbers from one to 10 are *wan, tu, tri, foa, faiv, sikis, seven, et, nain, ten*, with spelling based on the English phonetic interpretation of the pronunciation. "One hundred" is *wan handet* (HAN-dett), and "1,000" is *wan tausen* (TAU-ssen).

When referring to amounts of money, the time, and mathematics, the word denoting the cardinal number is used—for example, *nain kina* (NAIN KEE-nah), or "nine kina." When describing a number of anything else, the suffix *pela* (PEH-lah) is added—for example, *wanpela pikinini* (WAN-PEH-LA PEE-kee-nin-ee) means "one child," and *tripela meri* (TREE-PEH-LAH MEH-ree) means "three women." To describe ordinal numbers such as "first," "second," and "third," the word *namba* (NAM-bah) is placed before the cardinal number, as in *namba wan* (NAM-bah WAN) for "first," *namba tu* (NAM-bah TOO) for "second," and so on.

success is determined by the ease and enthusiasm with which the nation has adopted it. It has largely replaced Motu, the former lingua franca around the southern Papua area.

One of the features of Tok Pisin is its limited vocabulary. It has around 1,300 words that do the equivalent work of 6,000 words in English. This leads to ingenious combinations of words strung together to provide the clearest meaning. Take the body parts. Instead of a single word for "toe," Tok Pisin uses *pinga bilong lek* (PIN-gah BEE-long LEK), or "finger belonging to the leg," and the elbow is called *skru bilong han* (SKROO BEE-long HAN), or "screw belonging to the hand." While *kaikai* (KHAI-khai) means "food," "breakfast" is *kaikai bilong moningtaim* (KHAI-khai BEE-long MOH-ning-time), and "lunch" is *kaikai long belo* (KHAI-khai long BEH-loh). *Belo* means "bell," but *belo kaikai* means "food bell," signifying noon. Therefore *kaikai long belo* means "food for noon," or lunch. "Lunch" is also known as *liklik kaikai* (LIK-lik KHAI-khai), or "little food," or sometimes even just as *belo*. "Dinner" is *kaikai long nait* (KHAI-khai long nite). "Dessert" is *switkai* (SWIT-khai).

COUNTING THE PAPUA NEW GUINEAN WAY

Westerners take their decimal system for granted. In Papua New Guinea there are probably more than 50 traditional methods of counting, devised by individual groups for their own uses. The decimal method, based on units grouped into tens, has caused outright bafflement in some areas. People whose traditional systems are different do not easily grasp the modern mathematical concepts. In some areas no words exist beyond the first few numbers; any number greater than two or three becomes "some," with especially large numbers referred to as "many."

Whereas most worldwide mathematical systems count with a base of 10, some groups in Papua New Guinea have a base of two. After counting one and two, there is no three, so it is back to one again. One group has a counting base of 47, made up of 23 points on the right side of the body (consisting of fingers, toes, and joints) and another 23 on the left. The nose is the 47th point, after which the counting starts at one all over again.

Considerable confusion has arisen, especially in trade stores—local general stores—because the rural owners did not understand the percentage markup system that was based on a decimal concept and failed to charge a profit margin on their goods. Fortunately the use of simple pocket calculators accompanied by a few demonstrations has solved the problem.

A coffee planter deposits coins for his clan. The Western style of calculating caused quite a bit of difficulty for many of the locals when it was introduced into Papua New Guinea.

TELEVISION AND RADIO

Radio has been around for some time, and it is the principal medium for mass broadcasting in a country where information has traditionally been passed on orally. The National Broadcasting Corporation was set up in 1973, and it operates a national shortwave station, AM and FM radio stations out of Port Moresby (largely in English), and provincial services in Tok Pisin, Motu, and other regional languages. Most of the nation is able to receive these broadcasts, which offer regional, national, and sporting news; community announcements; religious programs; and

A Papua New Guinean catching the local news on television.

entertainment and local music. A commercial operator broadcasts Yumi FM in Tok Pisin and Nau FM, a Western-style station, in most provinces.

Papua New Guinea did not have its own television station until 1987, when broadcasting stations were established in Port Moresby, Lae, and other centers. Papua New Guinea has one free broadcast television station, EMTV. People with expensive satellite dishes or pay-cable television, however, are able to watch Australian, American, Indonesian, and Malaysian programs. Videos are also popular, and they are available from trade stores, hotels, and *kai* shops, or food stores. Despite television's popularity, television sets are still reasonably rare, with one set for every 77 people.

Papua New Guinea has had a postal system since 1886, when the SS *Victory* carried mail between Australia and New Guinea, primarily using an Australian stamp system. Papua and New Guinea issued their first stamp in 1952, and today Papua New Guinea's stamps feature traditional and community themes. An extensive postal system is in operation, but mail is not delivered to individual homes. Instead people collect their mail from post offices and regional post agencies set up in trade stores. Domestic mail is carried by air, sea, and road, and airmail carried within the country does not incur any extra fees. Delivery of mail, along with that of people and supplies, to remote areas is carried out by air.

The country's urban centers have a fully automated telephone system, while in the remote areas connections are powered by solar energy. The radiophone is operator-connected to the very remote areas. There are no area codes, with direct dialing between centers. Cell phone technology is taking off in Papua New Guinea, providing people with an expensive but important new means of communication. As of 2007 there were about 300,000 cell phone users.

NEWSPAPERS AND BOOKS

The country has two daily newspapers, both of which are foreign-owned, English-language publications. The oldest, the *Post Courier*, has a daily circulation of 28,900. The *National* is Malaysian owned and sells 24,200 copies daily. The *Wantok*, with a circulation of 14,000, is published weekly in Tok Pisin by Word Publishing, which was set up by the Catholic, Anglican, Lutheran, and United churches.

Reading is steadily becoming popular as more people proceed to higher levels of education. The availability of books is fair in urban centers, where bookshops, libraries, and schools are located, but accessibility is poor elsewhere. Many bookshops are owned by Christian organizations but stock a wide range of books, not just religious publications, in Tok Pisin or English. Many schools, organizations, and government offices maintain their own small library collections. There are significant research-level libraries at the universities, and the National Library Service collects books, photos, and items of national and historical interest. Under provincial government, the number of public libraries has dwindled through underfunding from 22 in 1978 to only 11.

A man ties up the stacks of newspapers waiting to be recycled.

ARTS

PAPUA NEW GUINEA'S ART FORMS are largely traditional and practiced in the course of daily living. In a climate where heat and moisture cause organic materials to decay rapidly, the emphasis is rarely on creating permanence. Much art is created where the process is as important as the final product so that, in some instances, the art is displayed only briefly before being washed away (as with body painting) or stored out of sight (as in art created as part of a ritual). The art expressed by the people is therefore often not labeled as art by its creators. It is closely entwined with religion, the songs and dances performed in festivals, and body adornment.

In modern Papua New Guinea an effort is being made to collect and catalog the richness of the nation's artworks. The National Museum and Art Gallery is in charge of administering the National Cultural (Preservation) Act. Artifacts more than 20 years old are not permitted to leave the country unless they are being sent to overseas museums that already have a good collection. The museum also advises people against selling their old cultural pieces to artifact buyers, and anyone who wishes to export such artifacts must obtain the permission of the museum.

The Institute of Papua New Guinea Studies conducts ongoing research into all facets of traditional culture. It makes archival recordings of traditional music, folklore, myths, and poetry and films local arts and crafts. The institute encourages the development of new works in the contemporary setting and is a major publisher of modern poetry, novels, plays, and discussion papers. The National School of Arts provides training in traditional and contemporary art at the university level.

Above: **Tree-bark cloth is made by beating sheets of bark between two large, rounded rocks until the bark thins, spreads out, and becomes more supple. In some areas men and women wear clothes made of the cloth. In other areas it is used much as a Western artist would use a piece of canvas.**

Opposite: **Traditionally carved pieces being sold in a craft store in Papua New Guinea.**

TRADITIONAL MUSIC

Singing, chanting, and dancing are integral parts of a villager's daily life. They remain essential elements of religious rituals and indispensable components of every festival. Various musical instruments accompany the singing and dancing, in both religious and secular applications. Drums are the main musical instruments used. Rhythmic drumming resounds at all celebrations, and the drums are artworks in themselves. The *kundu* (KUHN-doo), seen on the national coat of arms, is a small drum carved from a hollow wooden cylinder, narrow in the middle and wider at each end, resembling an hourglass. It is played with one hand. Lizard skin or snakeskin is stretched across one end of the drum. It often has a handle and may have seeds, feathers, or other kinds of ornamentation. The *garamut* (ga-rah-MUTT) drums, found along the Sepik, are larger and are made from tree trunks that have been hollowed.

Wind instruments are common throughout the country, varying widely in construction and the sounds produced. In one area of the

Sepik, a series of eight long conical horns are played in a ritual, each with a different plaintive honking note sounded by its player at the correct moment to create a hypnotic tune. In the highlands pottery flutes such as the ocarina, a globular clay flute, are made. Sacred flutes that are made in male and female pairs and are never played separately are usually saved for initiation rites. There is also a small flute played with the nose, and other types of flutes are made in various parts of the country from reeds or bamboo.

Horns and shells are sounded around the country; in some coastal areas they are used to send warnings or other messages up and down the coast. In some areas bullroarers, which are swung around on a length of cord, make a loud, eerie, resonant moaning hum. New Britain has a musical bow made from a strip of palm with a string of vine, and people in the highlands created a small harplike instrument. The *lanaut* (LAH-nowt) from New Ireland is played for its range of bird and other animal sounds.

Since the 1970s, music and the other arts have been arenas in which Papua New Guineans have struggled to reconcile the clash between traditional culture and the rapid onslaught of new ways. The government encourages the continuation and, in some cases, the revival of activities associated with traditional culture.

A Huli tribesman playing a sacred flute.

Most of the country's pop music was recorded in Rabaul, in East New Britain Province, until its two recording studios were destroyed by the 1994 volcanic eruptions. The National Capital District is the new center for musical recording.

CONTEMPORARY MUSIC AND THEATER

Music students at the National School of Arts study both Western and Melanesian instruments, and many have chosen to synthesize the two. The rock band Sanguma was the first to succeed with its Tok Pisin and Tok Ples songs and homegrown blend of traditional and contemporary Western instruments and rhythms. It was very popular both at home and internationally, paving the way for other popular Papua New Guinean artists such as George Telek, Patti Doi, Painim Wok, Barike, and Paramana Strangers. In Port Moresby private clubs play modern jazz or blues music, and there are discotheques in the larger towns.

Performing traditional songs and dances comes naturally to Papua New Guineans. Doing so on a modern stage, with the technicalities of sound, lighting, and script, however, is a relatively new medium for the people. In the 1970s and 1980s both the National Theater Company and the Raun Raun Theater took up the challenge.

The National Theater performs locally written plays and incorporates elements of traditional song, dance, and plays into its repertoire of puppet shows, dance productions, and folk and contemporary plays. Audiences include urban and rural dwellers, and the company has also performed

SPECIAL SOUNDS

The people of Papua New Guinea can create extraordinary sounds with their voices. Inspired largely by the forest, many groups have a characteristic sound, either as a warning or for celebration, which is picked up and repeated so that it resounds throughout the area. Near the Sepik, for instance, inhabitants can produce various froglike noises.

in international arts festivals, where it has been well received. Community participation is encouraged through workshops that teach traditional dances and theater skills and techniques.

The Raun Raun Theater, based in Goroka, aims to bring theater to several provinces—particularly to large villages whose residents would not ordinarily travel to the urban centers—and its mobile nature has allowed it to accommodate the special needs of the country. It has created its own theater school.

Both the National and the Raun Raun theaters invite local people to submit scripts and incorporate uniquely Papua New Guinean perspectives into these productions so that they are culturally meaningful to the participants and audiences. Even though this type of theater is new to Papua New Guinean audiences, the people relate easily to the theatrical medium because storytelling—verbally and via music and dance—has always been a feature of their lives.

CARVINGS AND PAINTINGS

Apart from spectacular and colorful body embellishment, some groups of Papua New Guineans practice the visual arts via carving and painting, using a variety of materials. The Hewa people from Southern Highlands Province make ocher paintings on flat sheets of bark. These are created to gain power over the ideas or animals represented on them, particularly before hunting. They are not displayed as decoration but instead are stored in small thatched shelters until they deteriorate.

People in other regions traditionally carved storyboards from fragile bark. Today they construct these in a sturdier manner, depicting various village events in relief. In Gulf Province, *gope* (GOH-peh) and *hohao* (HOH-how) boards are beautiful shield-shaped carvings traditionally kept in the men's houses. They were thought to contain the spirits of ancestors

A wood carver examines his completed work.

ART TABOOS

The production of carvings and paintings has traditionally been enshrouded by a number of taboos. These are observed to ensure that the relevant spirit can inhabit the artwork. Abstinence from certain foods or fasting may be required, and the artist generally cannot associate with women, who may have an adverse effect on the secret rituals and magic. The artist is highly respected for his role, both religious and as a recorder of myths and special events. Today much of the religious significance of art has been lost, and the carver or the painter may have other reasons for his work, especially that of trading for better income.

A man stands in front of a mural. The various human forms found on the mural are a modern depiction of art based on traditional subjects.

or heroes and guardians of the village, but they have lost much of their spiritual significance and today are made for tourists and in only a few communities. They are carved with stone axes from the old wood of canoes, with cassowary bones and shark teeth used to create the finer details, and colored with paints made from burnt shells (white), charcoal (black), and clays (reds and browns). Similar works are the relief-carved *kakame* (KAH-kah-meh) figures, traditionally connected with head-hunting for ritual purposes and historically kept along with the racks of head trophies in the men's houses.

The Sepik River is often called the River of Art. Along the river, many things used by the people daily are lavishly decorated. Canoes, for example, are carved with decorative prows representing animals or people. Spirit masks, shields, and other large carvings are everywhere, and even clay bowls and cooking pots are decorated. On the Trobriand (also known as Kiriwina) Islands, carving produces ornate and useful walking sticks, stools, and small tables, sometimes inlaid with mother-of-pearl. Shell jewelry, particularly if made from the valuable black coral, is popular in the coastal towns. The art of carving is displayed in finely crafted bowls made from dark wood polished painstakingly with a pig's tusk. The rims of some are patterned with the coastal themes of fish and turtles.

While some masks are custom-made for ceremonies, most are produced as ornaments in the modern society.

WEAPONS, SHIELDS, AND MASKS

The creation of decorative weapons, shields, and masks throughout Papua New Guinea demonstrates the fundamental link between art and daily living. Weapons and shields have long been decorated for ceremonial occasions, and they help create the fearsome look of a warrior in full regalia. Stone axes in the Mount Hagen region are worn across the back and are of ceremonial value only. Their slate blades are attached to the wooden handles with decorative woven-cane strips. Some stone axes are etched with geometric motifs.

Sharp bone daggers, including those made of the valued cassowary bone, are worn as ornamentation. The Huli make small picks tipped with the slicing claws of cassowaries. Spears are bedecked with a variety of fiber bindings, feathers, and shells, as well as with incised designs. Shields are endowed with a spiritual symbolism that is just as important as the physical task of defense. They are highly valued by Western art collectors, as special care is taken in the process of carving and decorating them.

The masks of Papua New Guinea show great diversity in styles and materials, which range from wood to turtle shell, and their size can range from 12 inches (30 cm) in length to a lofty 47 inches (119 cm). Masks from some areas look almost African, but the Sepik spirit masks are as distinctive as the rest of the carvings from that region. They are carved from wood, then covered in molded clay that has been embedded with teeth (mostly from pigs), hair, and shells. Some masks are used exclusively by male secret societies and may be woven from pith.

MALANGGAN MASKS AND SCULPTURE

The wooden *malanggan* (mah-LANG-gan) masks and sculptures of New Ireland are some of the larger and more ornate wooden carvings on the island. They are elaborate panels depicting totemic animals and human figures commemorating the dead. The word *malanggan* also refers to feasts and celebrations held at the end of the mourning period when the carvings are made. Traditionally only one man in the tribe is permitted to make or display these masks, and it is looked upon as a highly coveted and respected role. A *malanggan* feast is an important occasion during which traditional teachings are passed on, but because of Christian conversions and the social effects of cash cropping, it is now practiced almost exclusively around the Tabar Islands.

COLORFUL BILUMS

Bilums are the colorful woven net bags seen nearly everywhere in Papua New Guinea. They are traditionally made from natural materials such as rattan, dried leaves, grasses, and strong pandanus fiber. Modern materials such as plastic and nylon are increasingly being used, with an even more colorful result. The bags are strong and versatile and are used to carry anything from a baby to huge loads of firewood. The process of making them is time-consuming, and most of the weaving is done by women.

The weaving skills traditionally seen in the making of baskets have been adapted in the highlands to create modern woolen blankets, bags, and bedspreads.

The *bilum* can be stretched to carry enormous loads and supported by the head, leaving the hands free to perform other tasks.

LEISURE

IN A COUNTRY WHERE PEOPLE WORK LONG DAYS just to feed and clothe themselves, time for leisure is limited. When women are not busy gathering or preparing food or collecting water and firewood, they occupy themselves by making handicrafts. Recreation in the villages, therefore, takes place largely at the end of the day with family members talking, listening to stories, or relaxing around the fire before going to bed. The work of the men tends to be physically difficult but more sporadic than that of the women, so they often have more time during the day. In some areas men spend time congregating in the men's house, talking or just smoking tobacco or chewing betel nuts.

Papua New Guinean nationals have their famous *singsings* (SING-sings) to provide a welcome break from the routine of daily chores. A *singsing* is any large celebration that incorporates feasting, drumming, dancing, and as the name suggests, much singing. *Singsings* are celebrated all over the country and can last a few days.

Left: **Men escape the hustle and bustle of town to relax by a lake.**

Opposite: **Local girls playing chess after school. Many Western-influenced games are gaining popularity in Papua New Guinea.**

BETEL NUT CHEWING

Betel nut, or *buai*, is the green nutlike fruit of the areca palm, which is chewed for its mildly stimulant effect. This effect is increased with the addition of a lime powder that acts as a catalyst. People also chew the betel nut with sprigs of a bitter pepper plant to improve the flavor. The chemical reaction between the *buai* and the lime produces a bright red liquid accompanied by copious saliva. Indiscriminate spitting means that the red liquid often ends up on pavements around town. The long-term chewing of betel nut causes the mouth to be dyed a bright red, while the teeth are permanently blackened. The practice can lead to mouth cancer.

There are beliefs and customs that surround the betel nut. Some argue that without the lime, chewing the fibrous *buai* is a good way to clean teeth and freshen breath in areas where toothbrushes are not used. Because of the copious salivation, it is said that chewing *buai* allows a person to work long hours in the sun without drinking water. Sometimes betel nut will be offered and shared between two parties as a token of peace once a dispute has been settled.

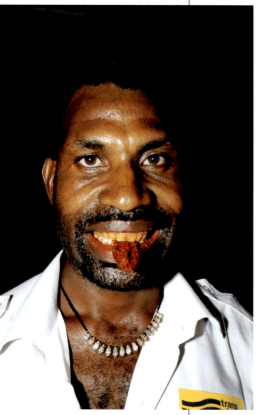

Many locals like this man enjoy chewing betel nuts. They are easily recognized by their bright red lips and mouth.

In some areas the plant has sacred uses as well. It is believed that the chewing of *buai* with ginger or some other herb can help a man chase away evil spirits if he spits while reciting magical words. In some traditions it is also believed that if a woman wishes to bear a son, she has to chew *buai* along with other herbs. At *singsings* the dancers will chew betel nut so that they can stay awake and continue dancing for many hours. It is believed that sorcerers can use the leftovers of a chewed betel nut to invoke magical spells that can cause death to the chewer. Those who

believe in such spells are very careful when disposing of their *buai* waste. In 1980 the Public Service Commission passed a ruling forbidding public servants from chewing betel nut at work or any time they are within a government building.

URBAN PURSUITS

Urban areas offer a range of activities beyond restaurants and private clubs, which are frequented only by expatriates and those with money. Small social gatherings among family and friends, with a meal included, are sometimes held—an urban version of the rural custom of gathering around the fire. Radio and television provide both entertainment and information for those with access to them, and movies are screened publicly in some towns.

Market days in the towns and the villages are opportunities to trade, shop, and talk with friends. Hotels and discotheques provide evening entertainment in the larger towns, although their numbers are limited. In the towns there are clubs for all sorts of outdoor activities including team sports, bush walking, sportfishing, boating, and diving.

SPORTS

The concept of team sports did not exist in Papua New Guinea before its colonization by the Europeans. Competitions in traditional skills—such as canoe races and displays of prowess in hunting, fishing, or other skills—were conducted by many groups, often associated with a *singsing* or a feast. The Christian missionaries introduced many team sports that required minimal equipment, and they were much enjoyed and rapidly gained popularity. As a result most of the sports played in Papua New Guinea have a foreign origin, although boating, swimming, and skin diving are not far removed from traditional activities.

Football refers to three separate games, of which rugby is the most popular. The play is rough, but no one seems to mind. Large games can turn into a sort of tribal warfare on the field and sometimes give vent to

Contact sports are quite dangerous for people who have suffered chronic malaria, as there is the risk of rupturing their enlarged spleens. However, this does nothing to dim the enthusiasm of Papuan New Guineans for playing football.

Baseball is one of the many outdoor sports played in Papua New Guinea.

underlying feelings of hostility. The spectators, who are passionate about supporting their favorite team, may join in, and violence can erupt. Rugby is played at the international, national, and local levels. Australian rules football, known as Aussie rules, also has its adherents in the country, as does soccer, which is sometimes called football as well.

Basketball, netball, softball, volleyball, and baseball are popular throughout the country, and these are sports in which women are more likely to participate. Other Western sports such as tennis, cricket, bicycle racing, and rock climbing are also enjoyed. As a member of the Commonwealth, Papua New Guinea teams can participate in the Commonwealth Games conducted every four years. Boxer Tumat Sogolik was the first sportsperson to win a medal for Papua New Guinea in the Commonwealth Games, in Edmonton, Canada, in 1978. The country's teams can take part in international sports events in Asia and the South Pacific as well.

Locals enjoying a game of volleyball on a beach in Papua New Guinea.

The Huli tribe lining up for their tribal dances during a *singsing*. This is an annual festival celebrating the clan in Papua New Guinea.

SINGSINGS

Singsings take place on all sorts of occasions—seasonal feasts, paying a bride price, initiation rites, traditional exchange ceremonies, even to celebrate the win of a favored politician. It is a chance for people to don their traditional finery and paint their bodies elaborately. Some of the feathers, magnificent headdresses, and shell jewelry worn are borrowed. New ones may also be made for special occasions.

The dances retell a traditional story or take on a new theme. Sometimes they are very heavily influenced by ritual; other times they can be more spontaneous. Preparation for the dancers can include fasting or restricting themselves to traditional foods, staying inside the village enclosure, and speaking only with the initiated men. Some parts of the *singsing* may have a more sacred significance, and women may be required to leave at that point. Some *singsings* are accompanied by the exchange of gifts.

ASARO MUDMEN AND HIGHLAND SHOWS

One famous legend enacted in Asaro *singsings* revolves around the mudmen. It is said that warriors of the Mut tribe were driven back by their enemies into the nearby river. They emerged later, ghostly pale due to their covering of dried mud. Their enemies mistook them for evil spirits and fled in terror. This legend is relived by the dancers, who cover their bodies in gray mud that, as it dries and flakes, represents the decaying flesh of the dead. Large rounded mud masks complete the illusion.

Highland shows, a variant of the *singsing*, are popular with residents and tourists. They are held in Mount Hagen and Goroka in August or September of alternate years. The shows were designed to demonstrate the similarities and positive qualities of the various highland groups and to foster goodwill toward strangers instead of suspicion and hostility.

In the early days of the highland shows, which started in the 1950s, as many as 40,000 warriors in full regalia would congregate and dance with their paints, feathers, and weapons flashing in the sun.

Mudmen from the village of Asaro, located in the Eastern Highlands province of Papua New Guinea.

FESTIVALS

PAPUA NEW GUINEA'S MOST WIDELY CELEBRATED festival is Independence Day, September 16. On that day celebrations and shows are staged throughout the country.

Seasonal festivals are held in various regions, such as the Yam Harvest Festival in the Trobriand Islands (June-July) and the Warwagira and National Mask festivals in Rabaul each July. The Hiri Moale Festival, held around Independence Day in Port Moresby, honors the ancient *hiri* trading voyages.

In addition to these regional festivities, villages and tribes celebrate their own festivals. Some of these are seasonal spiritual observances; others, such as the Tee in Enga Province and Moga in other highland areas, are special occasions where objects of wealth are ceremonially exchanged with neighboring or even enemy groups.

Left: **The tapioca dance performed by the men of the Trobriand Islands.**

Opposite: **Crowds gather to catch the dance site of the *singsing* in Garoka. Papua New Guinea's festivals call for large gatherings, colorful *singsings*, feasts, and parades. They are occasions in which people abandon their Western clothes to don traditional finery.**

One giant *lakatoi* sails from another island toward Port Moresby for the Hiri Moale Festival, which commemorates the annual trading voyages of the people's ancestors.

INDEPENDENCE DAY AND HIRI MOALE

Papua New Guineans celebrate their independence as a nation on September 16. While various ceremonies and shows are held all over the country, the biggest and most famous is the Hiri Moale, commemorating the ancient trading voyages made between villages in the Port Moresby area and Gulf Province.

Long before the arrival of Europeans, *hiri* were conducted amid ritual procedures. The Motu people in the Port Moresby area made clay cooking pots that they traded for sago in the Gulf Province villages, where sago was abundant. The voyages were necessary for the Motu because the dry climate of the Port Moresby area did not favor farming.

The building of the *hiri* canoes, called *lakatoi* (LAH-kah-toy-e), was supervised by two men who were honored by being selected for the role. During the building of the canoes, they had to observe strict taboos that involved eating special foods, not communicating with their wives in any way, and not washing or cutting their hair.

The canoes for the voyages had to be large and sturdy because they would traverse hundreds of miles with able-bodied men in them. Early in its construction, the bare shell of each boat was blessed by a shaman using specially concocted incense smoke. Village women plaited together strips of palm fronds for the sails, and these were then sewn together by the men. The sailors would depart in September, when the seas were calm and the winds most favorable. The villagers knew it would take at least 50 days before the winds changed to the northeast, enabling the sailors to return. A watch would be set up for the returning boats, and as the village waited in anticipation for their safe return, the people made preparations for a special homecoming feast.

The last *hiri* voyages were undertaken in the 1940s, but they are still honored. The festival provides an opportunity for people to gather as in earlier times and celebrate with canoe races, *singsings*, processions, competitions among string-based bands, and other contests.

Motu men were good sailors and had impressive boats with distinctive sails shaped like crab claws.

PUBLIC HOLIDAYS IN PAPUA NEW GUINEA

New Year's Day: January 1
Good Friday and Easter: March/April
Queen's Birthday: mid-June
Remembrance Day: July 23
Independence Day: September 16
Christmas Day: December 25
Boxing Day: December 26

In addition, each province has its own government holiday. These are usually observed on a Friday or a Monday to give workers a long weekend.

THE KULA RING

Another series of trading ceremonies involves a circle of islands, including the Trobriands, in and around Milne Bay Province. The early sea voyages by canoes are reenacted, although the distances covered today are not as lengthy as before. Modern vessels are sometimes used, but elaborately decorated canoes are still favored.

The exchange of goods serves the purpose of spreading goodwill among the islanders. The items exchanged are decoratively carved armbands and special necklaces called *bagi* (BAH-ghee), made with red shells that are painstakingly ground by women into evenly proportioned circular disks. The exchanges are purely ritualistic, and the goods rarely leave the trading ring. What is significant is that travelers are offered hospitality by their exchange partners. The armbands travel counterclockwise around the ring of islands, and the necklaces clockwise. The goods are passed through a complete circle in about five years. Besides the exchange of the ritual jewelry, it is also an important opportunity to trade in goods such as baskets, food, and pottery.

MUSIC AND MASKS IN RABAUL

People have gathered for the Warwagira Festival since 1971, and it features contests among choirs, string bands, theater groups, and traditional dance groups. It takes place every July and is closely followed by the National Mask Festival, first held in 1995, a year after Rabaul was devastated by volcanic eruption. It is a celebration of the nation's mask cultures. It features mask ceremonies with sacred life-size woven cane figures called *tambuan* and many mask dances.

EXCHANGE CEREMONIES: THE TEE AND MOGA

In some areas of Papua New Guinea, preparations for huge exchanges require several years between ceremonies. One reason is to collect the appropriate number of pigs. These ceremonies are sometimes held to exchange "payback goods," but more often they are designed to display the wealth of a "big man" or a clan.

One ceremony is held specifically to repay debts incurred and add items to the repayment. In most parts of the highlands the ceremonies are called Moga, while the Enga, from Enga Province in the highlands, have a similar custom called the Tee. These ceremonies are accompanied by all the trimmings of a *singsing*. Goods exchanged include pigs, kina shells, and even cartons of beer. Many pigs are slaughtered, and the feasting can continue for several days. The repetition of these exchanges means that at some point in time, the giver will get back things similar to what he has given and sometimes receive more. The larger exchanges can include not only gift giving and dancing but marriages and initiation ceremonies as well.

People gather to see the display of kina shells during an exchange ceremony.

The chief's yam house is always the first to be filled after a harvest.

TROBRIAND YAM HARVESTING

In the Trobriand Islands, the yams cultivated for food represent more than mere nourishment; people take pride in the size and quality of the yams they grow. The yams are a sort of status symbol and speak of the cultivator's farming skills. Men sometimes spend hours discussing the growing of yams, and it is an honor to be known as a good yam cultivator.

Yam harvesting takes place in July or August each year. As they are dug up, yams are displayed in gardens to be admired by all. The women flank the procession in which the yams are carried back to the village by the men. The yams are then displayed in circular piles and appreciated.

The village is arranged around the central yam houses. These form an inner ring that is surrounded by the sleeping houses, and these in turn are surrounded by trees. The yam houses are used for storage but remain open enough to display the number of yams inside.

A man has one yam house for each of his wives, and it is the responsibility of his wife's clan to fill that yam house, while the owner fills someone else's. Again there are rituals to be observed, and the chief's yam house is always the first to be filled. In this way the yams form an essential part of the ceremonial exchange that cements the ongoing relationship and goodwill among the islands' villages. The yam harvest and its accompanying celebrations can last up to three months. It is a time of much feasting, dancing, singing, and general festivities.

MAPRIK YAM FESTIVALS

The celebration of the yam harvest is observed differently by the Abelam in the Maprik region near the Sepik. Yams are the staple food there, grown on distinctive trellises. Sometimes the cultivation and harvest are the sole responsibility of the men, carried out in secrecy from the women. The yams are stored in special huts, but for the harvest festival the largest yams are collected amid much ritual and singing and decorated with woven masks or painted with faces so that they look like human figures.

In a good year, some of the yams will reach a spectacular 10 feet (3 m) in length, although usually the largest ones are about 6-7 feet (1.8–2.1 m) long. After the harvest has been praised and the celebrations accomplished, the displayed yams are presented to the women as gifts.

Men rejoicing in a village clearing after a successful yam harvest. The tall structures at the back are yam storage houses.

FOOD

UNLIKE MANY OTHER COUNTRIES, Papua New Guinea does not have a distinctive cuisine. There are no special ingredients or flavors to capture the attention of culinary experts around the world. Many people prepare food at the subsistence level, eating bland and unchanging diets based on sweet potatoes or sago for breakfast, lunch, and dinner.

No spices were used traditionally, although many are now grown as cash crops and are making their way into people's diets. Ginger is added to the cooking in some areas and is also sometimes put into freshly brewed black tea for drinking. Salt is used heavily throughout the country. It is added to food for flavor or used as a preservative when fresh meat is available.

Most diets are deficient in protein. Whenever possible, dietary protein is sourced by fishing in rivers and coastal areas, farming chickens for food, and hunting small marsupials. Hunting game birds is not a taboo along the Sepik River. Occasionally crocodile flesh is added to the menu.

Left: **A family preparing a home-cooked meal.**

Opposite: **Fresh-caught fish hanging from a pole in a market. Given the vast waters of Papua New Guinea, fish is one of the country's most popular meat foods.**

Pigs roasting on spits in preparation for a village feast.

The nation imports large quantities of canned fish and rice, which make a staple dish when mixed together. Sometimes only canned fish, rice, salt, and tobacco are available in trade stores. Pigs are kept as a symbol of status and not so much for their food value, though they are slaughtered on special occasions to provide the much-appreciated meat for the feast. Papua New Guineans grow a wide variety of tropical fruits and vegetables, and some even plant Western vegetables in their gardens.

Kitchens in the urban areas are set up in the Western style, with electric stoves, metal pots and pans, running water, storage cupboards, dishes, and silverware. In the rural areas, cooking is done over wood fires, either inside or outside the house. Sometimes there is a special open-sided *haus-wind* (HOWS-wind) hut, where the cooking fire is located. Unglazed clay pots are used for the cooking, while large feasts are prepared in ground ovens. Food is eaten from rough baskets, banana leaves, or coconut-shell halves. Metal pans are increasingly common where once only clay pots were available.

For large feasts, a clay ground oven called a *mumu* (MOO-moo) is used. This is essentially a hole in the earth lined with stones that have been heated for several hours by a well-fed fire. The size of the pit depends on the number of people being catered for—a few dozen or several hundred. A pig is an essential ingredient, along with yams or sweet potatoes. Other ingredients that are available may also be included. Cooking in a *mumu* is a slow process, and people often sing, dance, and tell stories while waiting for the food to cook. When ready, the cooked food is served to attendees in order of seniority on banana leaves.

The simplest and yet paradoxically most lavish cooking style in Papua New Guinea uses a ground oven. For feasts, the pit may be several hundred feet long and filled with hundreds of whole pigs.

A GROUND-OVEN FEAST

Fresh banana leaves (kitchen foil can be used as a substitute)
Fleshy young pandanus fruit (or small onions), peeled and left whole
Yams or sweet potatoes, chopped into chunks
Vegetables in season or pumpkin, cut into chunks
Pork, cut into large chunks
Green leafy vegetables

This makes a wonderful barbeque, but you will need adults to help you prepare the pit and hot stones.

Choose a dry area and dig a hole, then use coals to create a hot pit. Line the bottom and sides with banana leaves, and scatter handfuls of pandanus fruit or onions. Add a layer of yams or sweet potatoes, then a layer of seasonal vegetables or pumpkin. Add pork, then green leafy vegetables to simmer in the meat juice. Cover the food with another layer of banana leaves, and roll live coal over the top of the leaves, taking care not to burn yourself. Seal the oven with earth. After about two hours, remove the earth cover, put the coal aside, and share the food. The amount of food used and the cooking time vary according to the number of people being served.

It takes great skill to skin a crocodile so that the hide comes off in one piece. The hide is sold, while the flesh can be eaten.

HUNTING AND FISHING

Hunting is an activity enjoyed by the men. It also provides a valuable addition of nutrients to the diet, particularly in areas where the staple is sago, a crop that is not high in vitamins. Shotguns and rifles are increasingly common throughout the country and are more effective than traditional hunting weapons such as spears and bows and arrows. Wild pigs, wild dogs, bandicoots, tree possums, wallabies, and birds are favorite targets of the hunters. Great skill is required to find and hunt these animals, as they are often quite small.

It also takes great skill to hunt crocodiles because they are powerful and dangerous. At night, hunters reflect powerful flashlights into a crocodile's glowing eyes, thus dazzling it and allowing a hunting canoe to get close enough to kill it with a long harpoon, aided by a blow from an ax on a softer part of the armored creature's body. Sometimes guns are also used. During the day and in shallow water, pairs of skilled hunters search around slowly with their feet in the clay of the riverbed until they find the scaly hide of the smaller New Guinea crocodile. One hunter will suddenly duck underwater and pull the surprised and thrashing creature while the other uses a large, well-aimed knife to kill it. Crocodile skin is quite valuable, and the meat from a large crocodile can be enough to feed a whole village.

Fishing is carried out by ingenious methods. A large variety of fish and shellfish are caught and eaten, including crayfish, prawns, and crabs.

BREEDING CROCODILES

Overhunting has greatly reduced the number of crocodiles along the Sepik, and farming them is a profitable alternative. Instead of capturing the grown crocodiles, farmers leave them in the wild and collect younger crocodiles and eggs. Eggs are often laid on floating clumps of vegetation and guarded ferociously by their territorial mothers, so modern methods are used to gather them. A helicopter lowers by a rope a nimble individual who hastily collects several of the eggs before the mother has a chance to attack. The local landowners are paid for each egg collected on their land, providing a valuable source of income.

Spears along with bows and arrows are popular, while some fishers use nylon nets or fishing lines. In some areas huge basketlike fish traps, which are often larger than the fishermen, are woven. Smaller traps made of thorny materials are woven into a cone shape and baited. A fish that is drawn to the bait gets hooked on the thorns.

In other areas, a mild poison called rotenone, which paralyzes the respiratory system, is made by crushing a vine root. The poison is poured into the water, and the fishermen simply wait for the dead fish to float to the surface. In New Ireland, some men attract sharks to their canoes, with either their voices or a rattle made from coconut shells. A noose attached to a piece of wood is then slipped around the shark's body. Dragging this device slows the shark and tires it. Once the animal is sufficiently exhausted, it is speared or bludgeoned, but it often still puts up a fight while being hauled into the canoe.

Fish and other meats are eaten freshly cooked when possible, and any surplus is salted and dried or smoked over a slow fire. Cooking methods include slow baking in ground ovens, roasting over glowing coals, and boiling in a clay pot with water, sweet potatoes, and greens.

A vendor selling fresh fish at a market.

Women processing the sago palm to extract its starch flour.

SAGO AS A STAPLE FOOD

Sago, or *saksak* (SACK-sack) as it is called in Tok Pisin, is the starchy food eaten by all the groups of people who live in the swampy areas of the country, especially along the Sepik and its tributaries. It is a very bland and nearly pure starch, and while it provides energy, it lacks the vitamins and minerals that other plant foods provide. Sago is important because it grows in areas where it is nearly impossible to cultivate other crops because of frequent flooding and waterlogged soils.

The process of obtaining sago is a lengthy one. The sago palm grows for about 15 years, storing starch inside its trunk before it flowers—which it does only once in its life. It must be harvested at that point, or the starch will be converted into a massive spike of flowers, after which the palm will die. In the past, before the tree was chopped down a ceremony was conducted to appease the ancestor spirit believed to reside in every sago palm, but this is rarely done now.

The tree is cut down by men and dragged or floated closer to the village or to a convenient clearing, where the bark is stripped. The pith inside is chopped and pulped, again by men. The women beat and wash the pith repeatedly with water to extract the starch; the water is collected, and the starch forms a thick, gluey mass at the bottom. It is dried to form a flour that preserves well and is the basis of sago consumption.

There are three basic ways to prepare sago. The flour can be boiled in water—or the sago can be cooked immediately before it has dried into flour—to form a thick glutinous porridge to which fish, coconut, or vegetables are added. The second method is to mix the flour with a little water to form a thick pancake that is fried on both sides in a very hot pan without fat or oil. The third is to simply pour the sago into a hot pan. The sago hardens immediately and is flattened and turned over to cook on the other side. The resultant flat cakes are known as *parem* (PAH-rem) and tend to be crispy on the outside and soft and chewy on the inside. They are convenient, as people can carry them on their daily tasks and eat them when needed. In addition, sometimes people make sago dumplings to be eaten with vegetable soups.

Sago starch can be cooked in many ways.

SWEET POTATOES, YAMS, AND OTHER VEGETABLES

There are many varieties of sweet potatoes, differing in color, texture, size, and flavor. These are the staple carbohydrate source in many areas, particularly in the highlands. Sweet potatoes are quite nutritious but do not form a balanced diet in themselves. Known as *kaukau* (KOW-kow) in Tok Pisin, they can be roasted whole, cut up and boiled with meat and other vegetables, steamed with other food in banana leaves, or baked in a *mumu*.

Yams and sweet potatoes are staples in the people's diet.

While men may be involved in the initial preparation of the garden and even the planting of the *kaukau* and yams, it is the women who tend the gardens. The men prepare the fields for planting by cutting tree roots left in the field and digging the soil to loosen it. The women's work involves breaking up large pieces of earth and preparing mounds of the earth for planting. They then push pieces of *kaukau* or yam vine into the mounds, leaving a small part exposed. While waiting for the vines to grow the women have to attend to the weeding. In three or four months, new vines will spread and cover the ground; under the soil are new *kaukau* or yams to be harvested.

People tend to harvest only a few sweet potatoes at a time because the damp climate causes food in storage to rot readily. The importance of *kaukau* in the diet is reflected in the arrangement of the garden—other crops are never accorded more than a quarter of the cultivated land.

Some groups of sweet potato growers in the highlands have an efficient way to grow their crops despite the cooler temperatures. They build large, low mounds of soil over old vegetation, and these form the planting beds for the sweet potatoes. As the old vegetation decomposes, the compost adds vital nutrients to the soil in addition to raising the temperature of the mounds, thus protecting the plants on cold nights.

In a typical Papua New Guinean garden, you might find any of the following: three or four varieties of sweet potatoes, yams, taros, starchy bananas for cooking, peanuts, long green beans, local leafy green vegetables, corn, chilies, cassavas (whose roots yield the starchy tapioca), sugarcane, ginger, pumpkins, *pitpit* cane (the flower is edible), pandani, breadfruits, papayas, and even tobacco. There are often coconut palms nearby as well.

Many of these vegetables and fruits are cooked by the same methods as sweet potatoes, but the coconut is widely included in other mixes of food. Fresh green coconut is moist and creamy in flavor, unlike the desiccated variety found on supermarket shelves. It is commonly grated into a fine mash and added directly to the pot, or the grated coconut is wrapped in a piece of coarse cloth that is squeezed tightly to extract the milk from it. When coconut milk is added to the meal, especially to cooked rice, the food is rich in flavor.

THE VERSATILE FRUIT

Bananas are eaten all over Papua New Guinea. Approximately 870,000 tons (883,960,803 kg) are grown and consumed nationally each year, and more than 200 varieties are cultivated, some of which come in surprising colors like orange. They can be used as both fruit and vegetables, but there is a difference between the two. The sweet, ripe eating bananas, known as *swit banana* (SWIT bah-nah-nah) in Tok Pisin, have bigger ridges on the fruit. The green, starchy cooking bananas, known as *karapua* (kah-RAH-PU-ah), are longer and paler.

Rich in carbohydrates, cooking bananas are treated like a starchy vegetable and cannot be eaten raw. They can be roasted whole in their skin, baked with coconut milk, boiled and mashed, chopped and added to stews, or sliced thinly and fried in hot oil as chips. Sweet bananas are also cooked in dishes where a sweeter flavor is wanted, such as in curries, meat dishes, or desserts, but are often eaten raw.

Other parts of the banana plant are useful as well. Banana leaves are heated by moving them around in a flame or a hot stove until they are soft and pliable, and then they are used to wrap food prior to cooking. They impart a delicate flavor as well as preserve the tasty juices of the food that is being cooked. The male bud of the banana plant can be peeled and the inner part either sliced thinly and eaten raw or boiled as a vegetable.

CHICKEN IN COCONUT CREAM

2 tablespoons (30 ml) of cooking oil
1 chicken, cut into pieces
1 large sweet potato, peeled and cubed
1 large or 2 medium onions, chopped
3 cups (750 ml) of chopped vegetables (use a mix of what you have available, such as butternut squash, green beans, potatoes, fresh corn kernels, yams, or green cooking bananas)
2 cups (500 ml) of canned coconut cream
2 cloves of garlic, crushed
1 ½ (7.5 ml) teaspoons of grated ginger
Salt
Chopped chilies or curry powder to taste (optional)

Preheat oil in a large pot, then brown the chicken pieces. Add the sweet potato, onion, and the rest of the vegetables. Pour in the coconut cream, and stir to cover the meat and vegetables. Add garlic, ginger and salt to taste, and any additional seasonings.

Bring to a boil, then cook gently for 30–40 minutes, until all the vegetables are tender. Serve the meat and vegetables with some of the gravy poured over them.

SWEET POTATO BISCUITS

This is a recently introduced but popular recipe, using nontraditional ingredients such as flour, milk, and margarine. These "biscuits" would be referred to as "cookies" in the United States. What is called a "biscuit" in the United States is called a "scone" in Papua New Guinea.

1 cup (250 ml) of flour
1 teaspoon (5 ml) of baking powder
Pinch of salt
¼ cup (60 ml) of sugar
½ cup (125 ml) of cold, well-cooked sweet potato
1 tablespoon (15 ml) of milk
2 tablespoons (30 ml) of margarine

Sift the flour, baking powder, and salt. Add the sugar. Mash the sweet potato, milk, and margarine together thoroughly in a mixing bowl. Add the flour mixture into the sweet potato mixture and mix until it forms a soft dough. Take small spoonfuls of the dough and roll into balls. Place on a greased tray, and press them down lightly with a fork. Bake at 350° F (180° C) for around 15 minutes, or until golden brown. Allow to cool on a rack.

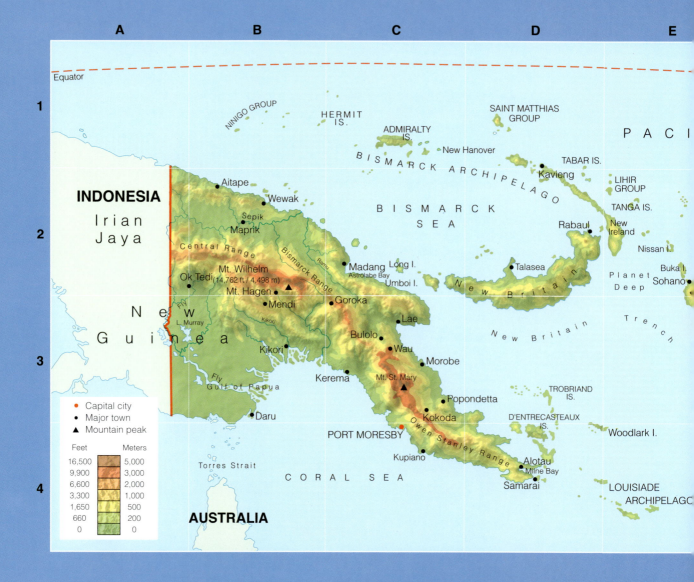

A   B   C   D   E

Equator

1

NINIGO GROUP

HERMIT IS.

ADMIRALTY IS.

SAINT MATTHIAS GROUP

New Hanover

TABAR IS.

Kavieng

P A C I

BISMARCK ARCHIPELAGO

LIHIR GROUP

TANGA IS.

INDONESIA

Aitape

Wewak

BISMARCK SEA

Rabaul

New Ireland

Nissan I.

**I r i a n
J a y a**

Sepik

Maprik

2

Central Range

Bismarck Range

Ramu

Long I.

Madang

Astrolabe Bay

Umboi I.

Talasea

N e w

B r i t a i n

P l a n e t
D e e p

Buka I.

Sohano

Ok Tedi

Mt. Wilhelm
(14,762 ft / 4,498 m)

Mt. Hagen

Fly

L. Murray

Mendi

Goroka

Lae

New Britain

T r e n c h

N e w

Kikori

Bulolo

Wau

Morobe

3

G u i n e a

Kikori

Kerema

Mt. St. Mary

TROBRIAND IS.

Fly

Gulf of Papua

Popondetta

Kokoda

D'ENTRECASTEAUX IS.

Woodlark I.

Daru

Capital city
● **Major town**
▲ **Mountain peak**

PORT MORESBY

Owen Stanley Range

Feet	Meters
16,500	5,000
9,900	3,000
6,600	2,000
3,300	1,000
1,650	500
660	200
0	0

Torres Strait

Kupiano

Alotau

Milne Bay

LOUISIADE ARCHIPELAGO

4

C O R A L   S E A

Samarai

AUSTRALIA

MAP OF PAPUA NEW GUINEA

Admiralty Islands, C1
Aitape, B2
Alotau, D4
Arawa, E3
Astrolabe Bay, C2
Australia, B4

Bismarck Archipelago,
C1–C2, D1–D2
Bismarck Range, B2, C2
Bougainville, E2–E3
Buka Island, E2
Bulolo, C3

Central Range, A2, B2
Coral Sea, B4, C4

Daru, B3
D'Entrecasteaux
Islands, D3–D4

Equator, A1, B1, C1,
D1, E1, F1

Fly River, A2, B2–B3

Goroka, C3
Gulf of Papua, B3

Hermit Islands, B1, C1

Indonesia, A1–A3
Irian Jaya, A1–A3

Kavieng, D1–D2
Kerema, C3
Kikori, B3
Kikori River, B3
Kokoda, C3
Kupiano, C4

Lae, C3
Lake Murray, A3, B3
Lihir Group, E2
Long Island, C2
Louisiade Archipelago,
D4, E4

Madang, C2
Maprik, B2
Mendi, B3
Milne Bay, D4
Morobe, C3
Mount Hagen, B2
Mount Saint Mary, C3
Mount Wilhelm, B2

New Britain, C2, D2-D3
New Britain Trench, C3,
D3, E3
New Guinea, A1–A3,
B2–B4
New Hanover, C1
New Ireland, D2, E2
Ninigo Group, B1
Nissan Island, E2

Ok Tedi, A2, B2
Owen Stanley Range,
C3–C4, D4

Pacific Ocean, E1–E2,
F1–F3
Planet Deep, E2–E3
Popondetta, C3
Port Moresby, C4
Rabaul, D2
Ramu River, B2,
C2–C3

Saint Matthias Group,
D1
Samarai, D4
Sepik River, B2
Sohano, E2
Solomon Islands,
F3–F4
Solomon Sea, E4, F4

Tabar Islands, D1–D2
Talasea, D2
Tanga Islands, E2
Torres Strait, B4
Trobriand Islands, D3
Umboi Island, C2

Wau, C3
Wewak, B2
Woodlark Island, D4,
E4

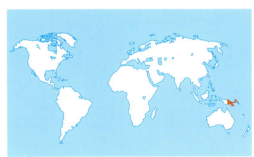

ECONOMIC PAPUA NEW GUINEA

Agriculture

 Coffee

Poultry

Vanilla

Manufacturing

Petroleum refinery

Cannery

Oil refinery

Sugar refinery

Services

Airport

Port

Hydroelectricity

Tourism

Natural Resources

Gold

Copper

Silver

Tuna

Oil

Lumber

ABOUT
THE ECONOMY

OVERVIEW

Papua New Guinea's economy relies heavily on income from mineral, oil and natural gas exports, and is vulnerable to fluctuations in global commodity prices. Fishing, forestry and agriculture are also important revenue sources, and a large portion of the population are non-waged subsistence farmers. Concerns over tribal violence, crime and corruption have limited the private sector and the country continues to be dependent on foreign aid.

GROSS DOMESTIC PRODUCT (GDP)

$4.438 billion (2007 est.)

GROSS NATIONAL INCOME PER CAPITA

$660

EXTERNAL DEBT

$1.814 billion

FOREIGN AID RECEIVED

$266.1 million (2005)

FOREIGN RESERVES

$1.664 billion

INFLATION (CONSUMER PRICES)

1.8 percent

CURRENCY

1 kina (K) = 100 toea (t)
K 3.03 = US$1

PERCENTAGE OF EXPORT INCOME

75 percent mineral, 19 percent agricultural
5 percent forestry, 1 percent marine products

MAJOR EXPORTS

Minerals, timber, coffee, palm oil, cocoa, copra

AGRICULTURAL PRODUCTS

Coffee, palm oil, cocoa, copra products, tea, rubber

MAJOR IMPORTS

Machinery and transportation equipment, basic manufactures (iron, steel), food and live animals, chemicals, manufactured goods.

MAIN TRADE PARTNERS

Exports to Australia 30.2 percent, Japan 8.2 percent, China 5.7 percent

INDUSTRY

Copra processing; palm-oil processing; plywood production; wood-chip production; mining of gold, silver, and copper; crude-oil production; petroleum refining; construction; tourism

WORKFORCE

3.557 million

UNEMPLOYMENT RATE

Total unemployment 1.9 percent
Urban unemployment as high as 80 percent

POPULATION BELOW POVERTY LINE

37 percent

CULTURAL PAPUA NEW GUINEA

Enga
Largest language group in Papua New Guinea; the Tee exchange ceremonies similar to the Moga ceremonies of Mendi.

Sepik River
Called the River of Art for its sacred masks, carvings, pottery, *haus tambarans* (spirit houses), canoes, totems, posts, and shields.

Mount Hagen
Annual Mount Hagen Festival, a gathering of thousands of highlanders in their spectacular traditional dress.

Goroka
Spectacular highland festival each August, and the Raun Raun Theater, the National Sports Institute, and the Melanesian Institute.

Asaro
Famous "mudmen" wear eerie gray masks made of mud to reenact a legend.

Rabaul
The National Mask Festival.

Baining Mountains
Fire dancing tradition in which people dance on hot coals wearing large, bark-cloth masks.

Lae
World War II memorial and cemetery in the botanical gardens; University of Technology; home to the Rainforest Habitat Zoo and Nature Park.

Mendi
Moga ceremonial exchanges of items of wealth, such as pigs and shells, accompanied by feasts and *singsings*.

Mount Giluwe
Papua New Guinea's tallest volcano.

Waigani
National Museum and Art Gallery, collecting contemporary and historical cultural artifacts and art; National Library; Parliament House, with its soaring *haus tambarans*–style roof and mural.

Port Moresby
Hiri Moale Festival, which honors the ancient canoe trading voyages, each September; University of Papua New Guinea.

Trobriand Islands
The Kula Ring, a series of ceremonial voyages to trade shell bracelets and necklaces around a ring of islands; yam houses and Yam Harvest Festival in July-August of each year; ruins of Polynesian stone temples on many islands.

ABOUT
THE CULTURE

OFFICIAL NAME
Independent State of Papua New Guinea

LOCAL NAME
Papuaniugini

NATIONAL SYMBOL
Bird of paradise perched on a kundu ceremonial drum, with a barbed spear behind the drum

NATIONAL FLAG
Diagonally divided from the top of the hoist to the bottom of the fly. The yellow bird of paradise is centered on the upper red triangle; the white Southern Cross constellation is centered on the lower black triangle.

NATIONAL ANTHEM
O Arise, All You Sons

LAND AREA
178,656 square miles (462,717 square km)

POPULATION
6.33 million

CAPITAL
Port Moresby

REGIONAL CENTERS
Lae, Madang, Wewak, Goroka

NATIONAL/OFFICIAL LANGUAGES
English is the official language; Tok Pisin and Motu are widely spoken.

TOTAL LANGUAGES
715 distinct language groups

ETHNIC GROUPS
Papuan, Melanesian, Negrito, Micronesian, Polynesian

FESTIVALS
Warwagira and National Mask festivals – July
Yam Harvest Festival – July/August
Hiri Moale Festival – September

LITERACY RATE
57 percent

LIFE EXPECTANCY
54 years

MAJOR RELIGION
Christianity

IMPORTANT HOLIDAYS
New Year's Day (January 1), Good Friday and Easter (March/April), Queen's Birthday (mid-June), Remembrance Day (July 23), Independence Day (September 16), Christmas Day (December 25), Boxing Day (December 26)

TIME LINE

IN PAPUA NEW GUINEA	IN THE WORLD

50,000 years ago
The first people are believed to arrive on the New Guinea mainland in the glacial period, as immigrants from the eastern Indonesian islands.

17,000 – 10,000 years ago
A gradual rise in sea levels covers the original land links with Australia.

A.D. 1526
Portuguese captain Jorge de Meneses sights the coast and names it Ilhas dos Papuas.

1546
The Spaniard Iñigo Ortiz de Retes lands on the northeastern part of the mainland and names the land Nueva Guinea.

1793
Britain claims the island of New Guinea and builds a fortified settlement, Fort Coronation. After trading for spices, dye roots, and teak for a year, the British abandon the settlement.

1828
The Dutch claim the western half of New Guinea with their settlement Fort du Bus, which they desert in 1835.

1884
Germany claims the northeastern area of New Guinea and the Bismarck Archipelago, setting up a trading colony administered by the New Guinea Kompagnie. The southeastern area of New Guinea is annexed by the British in the same year.

1906
The British protectorate is handed over to Australia and renamed Papua.

1914
Germany loses its colony when the area is occupied by Australian forces.

1921
The former German colony is renamed the Territory of New Guinea when Australia is given mandate over it by the League of Nations.

A.D. 600
Height of Mayan civilization

1000
The Chinese perfect gunpowder and begin to use it in warfare.

1558–1603
Reign of Elizabeth I of England

1776
U.S. Declaration of Independence

1861
The U.S. Civil War begins.

1914
World War I begins.

1939
World War II begins.

IN PAPUA NEW GUINEA	IN THE WORLD
1964 The First House of Assembly is formed, with 64 members.	
	1966 The Chinese Cultural Revolution
1968 The Second House of Assembly is formed, with 94 members who decide the independent country will be called Papua New Guinea.	
1973 On December 1, the territory obtains full self-government.	
1975 On September 16, the new constitution takes effect. Papua New Guinea is now an independent nation.	
1989 The Panguna mine closes due to attacks by the Bougainville Revolutionary Army, which is a disaster for the economy. A state of emergency is declared, and the situation deteriorates into civil war.	
	1991 Breakup of the Soviet Union
1997 Prime Minister Julius Chan secretly hires a mercenary group to fight the Bougainville insurgents. There is a huge outcry and rioting when the plan is leaked, and the prime minister and his deputy eventually resign. With international assistance, a cease-fire is negotiated.	**1997** Hong Kong is returned to China.
1998 A huge tsunami devastates the western coast of Sandaun Province, killing 1,640 people and making another 9,000 people homeless.	
2001 The Bougainville Peace Agreement is signed, with Bougainville given immediate but limited self-government.	**2001** Terrorists crash planes in New York, Washington, D.C., and Pennsylvania.
	2003 War in Iraq begins.
2005 On June 15, the new autonomous Bougainville government is sworn in, with Joseph Kabui as the first president. A referendum will be held in 2017 for a completely independent Bougainville.	

GLOSSARY

bilum (BILL-uhm)
Strong, woven string bag made and carried by women.

buai (BWAI)
Betel nut.

guvmen (GUV-men)
Government.

handet (HAN-dett)
Hundred.

haus tambarans (house TAM-bor-ans)
"Spirit house" storing items of cultural and religious significance.

hiri (hih-REE)
Ancient trading expedition.

kaikai (KHAI-khai)
Food.

kaukau (KOW-kow)
Sweet potato.

kundu (KUHN-doo)
Drum featured on Papua New Guinea's coat of arms.

kwik piksa leta (KWIK PIK-sa LET-tah)
"Quick picture letter"—in other words, a faxed letter.

laplap (LAP-lap)
Loincloth or piece of cloth.

luluai (loo-loo-AY)
Head man.

masalai (mass-ah-LAY)
Spirit.

Motu
Language originally used by the Motu people in the Port Moresby region, now more widely spoken.

mumu (MOO-moo)
Oven dug into the ground.

naiswan (NAIS-wan)
Expression of congratulations or approval, derived from the Australian phrase "nice one."

omak (OH-mak)
Kina shells worn on a length of string threaded between two holes in the shell and used in trade and barter.

parem (PAH-rem)
A sago pancake.

singsing (SING-sing)
Any large celebration with feasting, music, and dancing.

taul (TAH-ol)
Towel.

tausen (TAU-ssen)
Thousand.

Tok Pisin
The pidgin language spoken in Papua New Guinea.

Tok Ples
The native or local language.

wantok (WAN-tohk)
System of reciprocity that emphasizes sharing and mutual help among families, clans, or tribes; derived from the English phrase "one talk."

FURTHER INFORMATION

BOOKS

Carlson, Melody. *Notes from a Spinning Planet—Papua New Guinea*. Colorado: WaterBrook Press, 2007.

Connell, John. *Papua New Guinea*. London: Taylor & Francis, 2007.

Corazza, Jago. *The Last Man: Journey Among the Tribes of New Guinea*. Vercelli, Italy: White Star, 2008.

Montgomery, Sy. *Quest for the Tree Kangaroo: An Expedition to the Cloud Forest of New Guinea*. Boston: Houghton Mifflin, 2006.

Rannells, Jackson and Matatier, Elesallah. *PNG Fact Book: A One-Volume Encyclopedia of Papua New Guinea*. South Melbourne, Australia: Oxford University Press, 2005.

WEBSITES

Australian Screen. http://australianscreen.com.au/tags/Papua+New+Guinea/

BBC News: Country Profile—Papua New Guinea. http://news.bbc.co.uk/1/hi/world/asia-pacific/country_profiles/1246074.stm

CHM Supersound. www.chmsupersound.com/

Embassy of Papua New Guinea to the Americas. www.pngembassy.org/

Gallery-PNG. www.gallerypng.com.pg/

The Library of Congress: Portals to the World—Papua New Guinea. www.loc.gov/rr/international/asian/papuanewguinea/papuanewguinea.html

Music Samples of Papua New Guinea. www.scu.edu.au/schools/sass/music/musicarchive/PNGMusic.html

The National. www.thenational.com.pg/

Papua New Guinea Online. www.pngonline.gov.pg/

Papua New Guinea *Post-Courier*. www.postcourier.com.pg/

Papua New Guinea Tourism Promotion Authority. www.pngtourism.org.pg/index.html

Tok Pisin Translation, Resources, and Discussion. www.tok-pisin.com/

Tokpisin.net. http://tokpisin.net/

MUSIC

Telek, George. *Amette*. Shock, 2004.

FILMS

Connolly, Bob and Anderson, Robin. *Joe Leahy's Neighbours*. ABC DVD, 2005.

Owen, Chris. *Bridewealth for a Goddess*. Institute of Papua New Guinea Studies: Ronin Films, 1999.

Owen, Chris and Pike, Andrew. *Betelnut Bisnis: A Story from Papua New Guinea*. Civic Square: Ronin Films, 2004.

BIBLIOGRAPHY

Balzer, Trevor, et al. *Pidgin Phrasebook: Pidgin Languages of Oceania*. Hawthorn, Australia: Lonely Planet, 1999.

Burke, Andrew, et al. *Papua New Guinea and Solomon Island*. Footscray, Australia: Lonely Planet, 2005.

Gomez, Brian, ed. *Papua New Guinea Yearbook 2007*. Queensland, Australia: National and Cassowary Books, 2007.

Kavanamur, David, Charles Yala and Quinton Clements, eds. *Building a Nation in Papua New Guinea: Views of the Post-Independence Generation*. Canberra, Australia: Pandanus Books, 2003.

Nightingale, Neil. *New Guinea, an Island Apart*. London: BBC Books, 1992.

Rannells, Jackson and Matatier, Elesallah. *PNG Fact Book: A One-Volume Encyclopedia of Papua New Guinea*. South Melbourne, Australia: Oxford University Press, 2005.

Tawali, Sisilia. *Basic Cooking*. South Melbourne, Australia: Oxford University Press, 2006.

Turner, Mark. *Papua New Guinea: The Challenge of Independence*. Victoria, Australia: Penguin Books Australia, 1990.

Waiko, John Dademo. *A Short History of Papua New Guinea*. Melbourne, Australia: Oxford University Press, 1993.

Wheeler, Tony and Jon Murray. *Papua New Guinea, a Travel Survival Kit*. Melbourne, Australia: Lonely Planet Publications, 1993.

"Agriculture and Food—Papua New Guinea." 2003. EarthTrends Country Profiles. http://earthtrends.wri.org

"Art and Architecture, Oceanic." Encyclopædia Britannica Online. www.britannica.com

"Bougainville Readies for Autonomous Government." June 15, 2005. Australian Broadcasting Corporation. www.abc.net.au

"Papua New Guinea." CIA—The World Fact Book. https://www.cia.gov/library/publications/the-world-factbook/index.html

"Papua New Guinea" Embassy of Papua New Guinea to the Americas. www.pngembassy.org

"Papua New Guinea." Encyclopædia Britannica. www.library.eb.com.au

"Papua New Guinea." Europa World. www.europaworld.com

"Papua New Guinea." Statesman's Yearbook Online. www.statesmansyearbook.com

"Papua New Guinea." The World Almanac and Book of Facts 2007. www.sirs.com

"Papua New Guinea: Asia and the Pacific National Forestry Programmes." United Nations Food and Agriculture Organization. www.fao.org

"Papua New Guinea Cookbook of National Recipes." PNG Buai. www.pngbuai.com

Papua New Guinea Defence Force. www.defence.gov.pg/

Papua New Guinea Department of Minerals. www.mineral.gov.pg/

United Nations Department of Economic and Social Affairs. http://unstats.un.org

United Nations World Health Organization. www.wpro.who.int

"Warwagira and the Eighth National Mask Festival." Post Courier. www.postcourier.com.pg

INDEX

144